THE BIBLE IS TRUE

THE EWER

With alphabetic script round the neck, as found in fragments in the ruins of the small temple outside the walls of Tell Duweir (Lachish) (1295–1262 B.C.).

THE BIBLE IS TRUE

THE LESSONS OF THE 1925–1934 EXCAVATIONS
IN BIBLE LANDS SUMMARIZED AND EXPLAINED BY

SIR CHARLES MARSTON, F.S.A.

AUTHOR OF
"THE NEW KNOWLEDGE ABOUT THE OLD TESTAMENT"

THE RELIGIOUS BOOK CLUB
121 CHARING CROSS ROAD
LONDON

First Impression   .   .   *November* 1934
Second Impression   .   .   *December* 1934
Third Impression   .   .   . *April* 1935
Fourth Impression   .   .   *March* 1936
Fifth Impression   .   .   *December* 1937
Reprinted for the Religious Book Club   1938

Printed in Great Britain

PREFACE

Month by month archæologists continue to uncover secrets that were hidden several thousand years ago in the soil of Bible lands—of Palestine and Syria, of Egypt and Mesopotamia. Some of these discoveries throw light upon the earlier books of the Bible. A recent find has revealed the alphabetical script in use in Palestine immediately after the time of Moses. It definitely links up the writing found in Sinai with the Phœnician characters, and it would seem likely that the books of Genesis, Exodus, Leviticus, Numbers, Deuteronomy, and Joshua, were first written down in this script, soon after the events they purport to describe.

In consequence of such finds as these, *The New Knowledge about the Old Testament*, although published little more than a year ago, already requires a sequel, partly to record the fresh discoveries, and partly to revise previous conclusions in the light of them. The word "sequel" is used advisedly, for some of those archæological discoveries described in this earlier work are needed to complete the case presented for the reader's consideration in the present one, and no useful purpose would be served by re-editing this evidence.

Beside progress in archælogical discovery, further progress has been made in the examination of the

PREFACE

methods and assumptions of the so-called Higher
Criticism of the Bible. Some authorities have always
regarded these as unreliable, and contended that a
Court of Law would not recognize them. It will be
noticed how events have now justified this prediction.
The author is indebted to many archæologists and
scholars for the evidence cited in this volume, but these
are not to be held to assent to all the deductions and
conclusions of this book. They are concerned with
questions of fact, but where their statements involve
deductions, endeavours are usually made to quote their
actual words.

This work is the fruit of a lifetime of study of the
Bible, and conclusions concerning its contents, whether
critical or archæological. Active participation in
expeditions organized to dig in Bible lands began
in the year 1924, in connection with the Palestine
Exploration Fund's excavations on the hill of Ophel
outside Jerusalem. At that time, Professor Garstang was Director of Antiquities to the Palestine
Government, and the meeting that ensued led to the
organization of no less than five separate expeditions
to Jericho. The excavations made at this spot are
of the first importance, since they provide a key position
for Old Testament History. The author's thanks are
especially due to Professor Garstang, and to his devoted
wife, for their arduous work in the atmosphere, often
sultry, that exists at the foot of the deep Jordan valley.
For help in financing these five expeditions, thanks are
due to the late Lord Melchett, who bore half the cost

of one of them, and to Mr. Davis Bryan, the Musée du Louvre, the University of Liverpool, and the Leeds Philosophical and Literary Society, for collaboration in a later one.

Frequent references will be made to the invaluable work of Dr. Langdon, Professor of Assyriology at Oxford, and the expeditions of the Herbert Weld (for the University of Oxford) and Field Museum of Chicago. These expeditions have, for quite a number of years, excavated the site of the ancient city of Kish about eight miles east of Babylon.

A special debt of gratitude is due to Dr. Langdon, as a great scholar, as well as an excavator. It will be seen how his decipherment of quantities of cuneiform tablets enabled him to reach conclusions of fundamental importance. The erudition displayed in his monumental works—*The Venus Tablets of Ammizaduga*, which he wrote in conjunction with Dr. J. K. Fotheringham, the distinguished astronomer, and *Semitic Mythology* (vol. v. in *The Mythology of All Races*)—entitle him to rank among the forefront of many generations of Oxford's most learned professors.

The splendid achievements of Dr. Woolley in his excavations at Ur of the Chaldees, and the financial support from the British Museum and the University of Pennsylvania that rendered them possible, are also gratefully recognized. Such contributions from Mesopotamia are essential for the elucidation of the Book of Genesis, and indeed for all the earlier books of the Bible.

PREFACE

It has not been the good fortune of the writer of these lines to meet that distinguished American excavator, Dr. W. F. Albright, whose fame is great as an authority on recent Palestine archæology. His book, *The Archæology of Palestine and the Bible*, contains a record of the evidences he has found, left behind by those who lived in early Bible days. Some of these will be cited as occasion requires in these pages. They are the more valuable because Dr. Albright considers them from a different standpoint from that adopted in this book.

Thanks are also due to M. Charles Virolleaud, and that brilliant band of French archæologists who discovered and deciphered the Ras Shamra tablets. Associated with the latter work, mention must be made of M. Bauer of Halle, and M. René Dussaud. Some of the information concerning the contents of these tablets has been supplied by Mr. Theodor Gaster of London, who has had the opportunity of studying the originals in the Louvre Museum, Paris.

Yet again, much of the important evidence in this volume has been brought to light by the labours of our veteran British excavator and Egyptologist, Sir Flinders Petrie. Instead of resting on his well-earned laurels, he, in company with his devoted wife, has been engaged in solving the problem of the Hyksos or Shepherd Kings' civilization, by excavations along the Palestine side of the Egyptian frontier. Few realize how much Biblical archæology owes to Sir Flinders. The many references to his labours in this book give but a small conception of his achievements.

PREFACE

During the last two years the Wellcome Archælogical Research Expedition to the Near East, under the leadership of Mr. J. L. Starkey, has been making surprising progress in the excavation of the great mound of Tell Duweir, believed to be the site of the important Biblical city of Lachish. The evidence already derived from these excavations constitutes an important feature in this book.

The author's thanks are also due to the Palestine Exploration Fund, who, under the leadership of Sir Charles Close, are displaying renewed activities, and mention must also be made of the British School of Archæology in Jerusalem.

A debt of gratitude is due to Colonel Meinertzhagen, D.S.O., for supplying the unique extract from his diary which records his entry into the cave of Machpelah.

Considerations of space alone prevent the mention of other excavators in Bible lands, to whom the author is indebted for evidence used in the composition of this book, as well as to the researches of many of the leading scholars in all parts of the world.

Many of the quotations from the Bible in the ensuing pages are taken from the Revised Version.

CHARLES MARSTON.

November 1934.

CONTENTS

xi

CONTENTS

xii

LIST OF ILLUSTRATIONS

xiii

LIST OF ILLUSTRATIONS

MAPS

xiv

THE BIBLE IS TRUE

I

IN SEARCH OF REALITY

D URING the past four centuries, since Caxton introduced the printing press into England, the Bible has formed the basis of the learning of our race, the guide to our ethics, and is said to have been the source of our strength. To-day complaints are made that there is a growing neglect of Bible study, even among the clergy, and a tendency to disregard its ethics. The reason is ascribed to the fact that we live in an age in which material knowledge has greatly increased, and in which people express a desire for reality. They are no longer content to take the traditional beliefs on trust.

There is a sharp contrast between the reverence of the Victorian age for the Bible and the popular attitude to-day. Mr. Gladstone called the Bible "the impregnable Rock of Holy Scripture." To-day, Mr. Bernard Shaw calls it an old collection of myths and fairy-tales, and no serious protest appears to have been made. Which is right, Mr. Gladstone or Mr. Bernard Shaw?

Before entering into a detailed examination of this

question, let us go over evidence of a general character. Queen Victoria is said to have ascribed the greatness of our race to the Bible. Until recently at any rate, that has been the belief of many of our noblest minds. There is certainly some influence, above and beyond the capacities of our countrymen, which has enabled this little Island to play the leading part in the world.

It is also claimed that the wonderful material civilization which the United States and Canada have developed and enjoyed, sprang from the work of men who were devout believers in the Bible. Certainly the hardships and privations which Anglo-Saxon colonists once had to endure there, required almost superhuman courage and fortitude. Let us recall the pitifully inadequate tools and weapons with which they established themselves in a primeval wilderness, and faced the problems of orderly development in a land which had never known civilization. Britain and its Dominions beyond the seas, with the United States of America, have for centuries been the Bible-reading nations. So it is hard to believe that all this great civilization, and the benefits which it has conferred upon humanity, sprang from a book which was only an old collection of myths and legends.

Or again, let us remember that the Old Testament constitutes the very title-deeds of the Jewish race. Scattered abroad throughout the world, homeless, oppressed, and persecuted for eighteen hundred years, the Jews still exist as a distinct race. Had they perished in their numberless calamities and vicissitudes, it might

2

be said to-day, with some reason, that their title-deeds were vain, and that the Old Testament prophecies were of no account. But the continued existence and present prosperity of the Jewish race, is a cogent testimony for the truth of these prophecies, and so likewise is their present return to the Promised Land.

Thus, the witness of nations constitutes impressive evidence in favour of the Bible. Again, if we consider the New Testament in the light of what has happened since the time of Christ, it is hard for an unprejudiced mind to say that events have demonstrated any of its contents to be untrue. We are, of course, aware that many passages led believers to expect the early return of Christ. But Jesus Himself, when on earth, solemnly affirmed that He did not know when this should take place (Matt. xxiv. 36, Mark xiii. 32). He stated that His Gospel must first be preached among all nations (Mark xiii. 10). So far as we are aware, this condition has not yet been completely fulfilled.

Again, it is promised that His Coming is to end War. It is significant that despite the efforts of the League of Nations, and despite the awful calamities which everyone knows must attend another great conflict, the abolition of war is not yet assured. When we contemplate the plight of people to-day, we feel that despite the great material progress that has been made, despite the great advance of Science, real happiness seems lacking in our civilization. Throughout the world confidence has been shaken; we know not what a day may bring forth! Even as the Jews are fulfilling the prophecies of the Old Testament, it is not so incredible, as it sounds, to hear some people affirm that other nations are fulfilling those of the New Testament. Those who seek Reality must admit that general considerations such as these constitute evidence, not lightly to be disregarded, for the integrity of the Bible.

The case for the other side may be briefly stated in some such terms as the following: Science has proved the Bible to be wrong, and the witnesses that Science is right, are before us every day of our lives. They are tangible witnesses that do not tax our credulity. Look at our motor-cars and bicycles, look at our radios and aeroplanes, look at our electric lights and refrigerators, and a hundred other inventions of modern life; all the outcome of Science! They are reminding us all the time that Science deals with reality, and that where our forefathers trusted to the Bible, we may trust to Science. Has not the scholastic world, with the aid of Science, proved that the earlier books of the Old Testament were not written by Moses at all, but were in the nature of folk-lore and legends, handed down by word of mouth, and first committed to writing many centuries after Moses' time? Why, your own Church Commentaries tell us so! And while they still try to represent the New Testament to be correct, yet many of your clergy admit there are also scientific doubts about the Divinity of Christ, and His Resurrection, for Science has long since shown that all those miracles recorded in the Bible could never have taken place.

4

Plain speaking like this is favoured because it is thought to represent reality. There is much to be said for it; and such arguments as these certainly need examination, before we pass to the consideration of archæological evidence. It will be observed that an indiscriminate use is made of the word "Science," and that witnesses for the correctness of Science are motorcars and bicycles, radios and aeroplanes and the like. But bicycles and motor-cars and the other inventions enumerated, did not spring fully fledged and mature from the intelligence of a body of scientists. They were slowly and painfully built up, the product of a multitude of brains, some of which knew nothing about Science or its laws. The correctness of each idea as it took shape, could be and was verified by experience, and at every step and every stage of the development of the model, experience was both the judge of its correctness, and the guide to further modifications and developments. So it is always with inventions. The shelves of the Patent Office are crowded with a hundred thousand, and more, specifications of inventions describing ingenious devices, which have been abandoned because they have not stood the test or trial of experience; and let us remember that these Patent Office failures were usually based on some recognized fact. So it is obvious that the Science which is credited with producing these witnesses to testify to its excellency, was moulded and shaped with the aid of concrete facts of experience from start to finish.

But there are other Sciences which have had so little

contact with experience that their teachings do not possess the certainty of Mechanics or Electricity; and even the Sciences of Chemistry and Physics, which have had any amount of contact with experience, have both recently had to undergo considerable modification. For example, Einstein's Theory of Relativity has completely revolutionized the Science of Physics.

Again, the word "Science" is applied to highly speculative theories, which have little or no basis in fact, and whose verification is extremely difficult. So the identification of the word "Science" with Reality, in the present state of human knowledge is entirely erroneous; and the analogies of motor-cars and bicycles, radios, aeroplanes and electric inventions, completely fall to the ground. For the word "Science," although it represents much that is true, also shields much that is doubtful, and much that is altogether false. Analogies based on the Sciences of Mechanics or Engineering, or of Electricity, cannot yet be used by those who desire reality, to justify an assertion that Science has shown the Bible to be false. For it may well be that the particular kind of Science involved is itself at fault, and its conclusions of no account. Examples of this are given in the next chapter.

On the other hand, evidence of a kind similar to that which brought into being, and made possible, all these mechanical and electrical inventions, is now being turned up by excavators in Bible lands. In other words, it is material evidence left behind by men who lived in the days of Noah, or Abraham, or Moses, or Joshua, and the problem is how to put it all together and compare it with the Old Testament. Before we proceed to examine it, let us pass to some other considerations.

There are in this country, as elsewhere, numbers of persons who believe in the word-for-word correctness of the English Bible; and because people are prone to swing from one extreme to the other, it may be that this attitude of mind has led others to discard the book altogether.

Now, no matter what attitude (conservative or advanced) a man may adopt, he has to face the fact that there are sentences in the Bible which do not make sense. On the other hand such examples serve to demonstrate its great age. The same characteristic occurs in less ancient writings—even in the works of Shakespeare, composed only some three centuries or so ago, and in the English language. But the Bible, so far as the New Testament is concerned, was written down more than eighteen hundred years ago in the colloquial Greek of that time; while the Old Testament was composed from two thousand five hundred to three thousand five hundred years ago, in the ancient Hebrew language.

There seems abundant evidence that, in course of ages, little mistakes have been made by scribes in copying the sacred texts. But it would seem as though these only affect minor details, and do not alter the general sense of the narrative. In the case of the Old

Testament those acquainted with the Hebrew alphabet will be aware that it has no vowel sounds. Some of its letters so closely resemble others that mistakes in transmission are easy; and a comparison with the Septuagint, or Greek translation of the Hebrew text made three centuries before Christ, suggests that such mistakes have occurred even since that time. There have indeed been commentators who regarded the Septuagint as the more correct version of the text, on the ground that it was generally quoted in the New Testament, and was always used by the primitive Christian Church. Such considerations weigh against the assumption of the word-for-word and letter-for-letter correctness of the English Bible.

We must next allow for modern ignorance of the circumstances and surroundings of incidents described, or of words uttered, as recorded in the Bible. A knowledge of conditions in Bible lands, as they exist to-day, is needed in order to fully appreciate the setting and life of the Old Testament. If we are studying real History, we must expect to find examples of religious fanaticism which do not accord with Christian precepts. Moreover, those whose feelings are harrowed by the accounts of Old Testament atrocities should not forget that such incidents occur even in this enlightened age.

Again, when one reads of some event which does not accord with our conventional experience of the laws of Nature, it is only fair to remember how unconventional experiences, otherwise miracles, are recorded so frequently in modern life that some of them are probably true. And further, that present-day Science is no longer ready to dogmatize as to what is possible and impossible. There is yet another aspect of the miraculous which deserves our consideration. Suppose the critics of only fifty years ago had come across a statement that when the Law was proclaimed from Mount Sinai, the words were heard a thousand miles away; or that when the Queen of Sheba returned to her home in South Arabia, King Solomon arranged for her to hear there, the singing of the Psalms in his Temple at Jerusalem. Let us imagine the incredulity and scorn that would have been poured upon such statements!

To-day such stupendous miracles have become common experiences. Americans listen through three thousand miles of space to a speech of King George, or enjoy a European concert. Thus miracles may be, after all, largely a question of knowledge and ignorance. Times have been so bad, so much of our modern philosophy has let us down, that we are all more ready to admit the possibility of gaps in modern knowledge than we were a few years ago.

Those who employ critical methods in the study of the Bible, have often acquired the habit of representing those who disagree with them as suffering from prejudice in their outlook. But is there any reason why those who are led by evidence to adopt an orthodox attitude to the Bible, should be more prejudiced than those who describe it as a collection of fairy-tales? Come to think of it—the realistic way the Bible handles human nature and its infirmities, has always aroused grave antagonism. There are some who seek to justify their lives by casting doubt on the Bible. In a quest for the real truth one must surely take account of possible prejudices on both sides, and a long-standing accumulation of them.

There is yet another class of prejudice which the archæologist has to face; it comes from those who cannot disentangle themselves from their critical environment. Thus, when Schliemann uncovered the remains of Troy in 1870, the scholars laughed him to scorn. Or again: so bewildered were German professors when Dr. Hilprecht, on behalf of the University of Pennsylvania, laid bare a great temple platform at Nippur in Mesopotamia, built of bricks inscribed with the name of a monarch whom the critics had treated as mythical, that the excavator was positively accused of perpetrating the forgery of a whole Babylonian temple platform!

A charge of credulity is also brought against those who pay respect to the Bible. Yet people accept without a murmur many of the speculations of modern writers. Even a learned bishop has been heard to assert that we know now the world was created between four and five thousand million years ago! And it is no uncommon thing to read in the Press of the discovery of human remains one hundred thousand years old! When we come to consider how scanty is still our knowledge of the last five thousand years of human existence, these vast periods of time arouse our scepticism. They really impose a far greater strain on our credulity than do any traditional beliefs.

Although this book will draw attention to fundamental mistakes about the Bible, the author dares not make any claim to infallibility. There has been, and there is, every excuse for errors; but none for the positive assurance with which some were presented to the public; nor for the contemptuous disregard of the Bible narrative. The spirit which has led some commentators to strain at a gnat in the sacred text, and swallow a camel of conjecture, is void of all sense of proportion.

To-day, it ought to be the object of all educated and intelligent men and women to seek the Truth; and, having regard to the great part the Bible has played in our history, to accord it fair play. The perplexities of modern life may still, perchance, be solved, and fears and anxieties dispersed, by the reading and study of the Scriptures, even as our forefathers found to be the case.

II

CLEARING THE GROUND

IN order that the new Bible evidence may be considered with unbiased mind, some reference must first be made to the work of the so-called scientific criticism of the Bible. This course is necessary because the results conflict, and in any attempts to reconcile them the archæological evidence has to be obscured and often deprived of its full value.

The scientific criticism divides itself into two parts, the literary criticism, and the historical criticism; which together, known as the Higher Criticism, have arrived at certain conclusions. Adequate reasons must now be given why this criticism up to the present is untrustworthy and unreliable. It is with no desire for controversy that these reasons must be published, or that the author presumes to differ from past conclusions of learned professors. But since this work is written in order to further reality in our religious outlook, critics are not entitled to more consideration than traditionalists. It will be noticed that the results of the ensuing examination into the methods and assumptions of the Higher Criticism, affects this system's work on other books of the Old and New Testaments.

CLEARING THE GROUND

We are indebted to the *Encyclopædia Britannica* for the following extract from their article on the Bible:

Textual Criticism

"The aim of scientific Old Testament criticism is to obtain, through discrimination between truth and error, a full appreciation of the literature which constitutes the Old Testament, of the life out of which it grew, and the secret of the influence which these have exerted and still exert. For such an appreciation many things are needed; and the branches of Old Testament criticism are correspondingly numerous. It is necessary in the first instance to detect the errors which have crept into the text in the course of its transmission, and to recover, so far as possible, the text in its original form; this is the task of *Textual*, or as it is sometimes called in contradistinction to another branch, *Lower Criticism*. It then becomes the task of critical exegesis to interpret the text thus recovered so as to bring out the meaning intended by the original authors. This *Higher Criticism* partakes of two characters, literary and historical. One branch seeks to determine the scope, purpose and character of the various books of the Old Testament, the times in and conditions under which they were written, whether they are severally the work of a single author or of several, whether they embody earlier sources and, if so, the character of these, and the conditions under which they have reached us, whether altered and, if altered, how; this is *Literary Criticism*. A further task is to estimate the value of this literature as evidence for the history of Israel, to determine, as far as possible, whether such parts of the literature as are contemporary with the time prescribed present correct, or whether in any respect one-sided or biased or otherwise incorrect, descriptions; and again, how far the literature that relates the story of long past periods has drawn upon trustworthy records, and how far it is possible to extract historical truth from traditions (such as those of the Pentateuch) that present, owing to gradual accretions and modifications of intervening generations, a composite picture of the period described, or from a work such as Chronicles, which narrates the past under the influence of the conception that the institutions and ideas of the present must have been established and current in the past; all this falls under *Historical Criticism*, which, on its constructive side, must avail itself of all available and well-sifted evidence, whether derived from the Old Testament or elsewhere, for its presentation of the history of Israel—its ultimate purpose. Finally, by comparing the results of this criticism as a whole, we have to determine, by observing its growth and comparing it with others, the essential character of the religion of Israel." (*Encyclopædia Britannica* (13th Edition), vol. iii., pp. 857 and 858.)

The feelings first derived from reading this passage are those of hearty approval, and agreement with the aims and objects of this Criticism, and with its course of procedure. There comes also a sense of admiration for those engaged in the work. Fine fellows these Higher Critics—think of the erudition and knowledge, the familiarity with long-dead languages, and the understanding of what really did happen in Old Testament times! Think of the acumen and balanced judgments, the unerring instincts and freedom from all prejudice! We take for granted that men with all these endowments have been found, because

14

sure and certain results have flowed from their work
by these methods. That means, of course, those
critical conclusions which are now accepted by many
of the leading clergy in substitution for traditional
beliefs.

Such is the train of thought aroused by reading this
excellently expressed passage. It takes both time and
consideration to estimate the possibilities of the procedure there set out, and to decide upon its true value.
Careful and unbiased estimation, however, suggests,
that this Criticism presumes a state of knowledge,
whether linguistic or historical, more complete, judging
by the past few years' experience at any rate, than
scholarship possessed. It is also evident that those who
undertook the work—the Higher Critics themselves—
needed some source at which they could readily check
and verify their judgments step by step, one at a time,
each before they proceeded to the next one. Some
such guide to truth seems to us to-day to have been
essential; for with the best intentions in the world, in
such subjects as these, it is hard to discriminate between
truth and error, between what is a real fact and what
is only a fancy; and it is further necessary to bear in
mind that one single mistake carried consequences
that might vitiate all subsequent conclusions. The
scientists who were concerned in the development of
mechanics, or of electricity, or of chemistry, or even
of physics, had decided advantages over the critics,
for at every stage in their work they could test the
truth, or otherwise, of their studies by actual observa-

tion in the realm of experience. But this so-called Scientific Criticism was a device that dispensed with it.

Indeed it was a devastating argument against the system of Textual Criticism when it was claimed that it could not be applied to modern literature. The leading articles in *The Times* are the work of various writers, but are doubtless amended and corrected by editors and sub-editors. Textual critics did not pretend to be able to distinguish one writer from another, nor to isolate the emendations of the editor. Yet unless Textual Criticism could be used to analyse modern literature, how could it be correctly applied to documents composed more than two thousand years ago, and written in a dead language? It really seems as though the very fact that the documents were so ancient, and the language so old, created and caused the superstition that the critics could do so, and inspired their supreme confidence. If literary critics could have verified their system, step by step, with the aid of modern writings, then outsiders would have had more confidence, although the critics themselves might have had less. But the only verification that could readily be applied to Old Testament criticism, was the plain common-sense meaning of the text, and of tradition. Where these differed from the critical interpretations, they were designated as being "untrustworthy," or "unreliable," or "the insertion of a much later writer." In the case of modern literature the truth or otherwise of such slanders could be tested.

16

Even one of the best-known steps along the path of this literary criticism of the Old Testament is an uncertain one. Because different names for God are used in the earlier books of the Old Testament, because there is a great deal of repetition in the narrative, it has been assumed that these books are made up of different documents, loosely put together in the form of a literary patchwork or polyglot. So there have been evolved at least three unknown authors: J for the one who used the Jehovah name for the Deity; E for the one who used Elohim; and a third author P, who dealt with priestly matters, and seemed to use both the Divine names. Then the work of each author was isolated from the main text, and conclusions drawn. The process is fascinating, but how far is it all fanciful? Could it not be assumed *that even this book* is the work of three authors, and then dissected into three documents? And it must further be borne in mind that it is a marked characteristic of very ancient writings to repeat themselves, and to use diverse names for the Deity. The Ras Shamra writings, documents referred to later, actually contemporary with Joshua in their date, are an example.

But let us assume that the Pentateuch is based on documents, and that those documents have even been revised at various times in Jewish history. So far from making the critical task easier, it would seem to make it more difficult. To get behind such revisions, to break up sentences, and to assign them to different

writers, *to date these original sources*; and then to pronounce with certainty, all manner of things directly
contrary to the complete text, surely this is quite out
of harmony with scientific practice as conducted to-day
in other fields of research.

Authorities, like the late Professor Sayce, who felt
the force of these arguments, used to affirm that
such literary criticism would not be recognized in a
Court of Law; and this prediction has proved to be
correct.

In the year 1931, a Canadian lady, Miss Florence
Deeks, brought an action in the Canadian Law Courts
against the well-known writer, Mr. H. G. Wells, and
the Macmillan Publishing Company, for plagiarism.
Miss Deeks claimed that with the connivance of the
Macmillan Company, to whose Canadian branch she
had submitted the manuscript of a book called *The
Web*, Mr. Wells must have had access to her book, for
he had used considerable portions of it in his book
The Outline of History.

Mr. Wells, on the other hand, denied that he had
any knowledge of *The Web*; he stated that he had
never seen the manuscript of it; and had never used
any portion of its contents. In like manner the Macmillan Company pleaded in denial that they had
never broken faith with Miss Deeks, by permitting
anyone to have access to *The Web* while it was in their
custody; and they affirmed that her manuscript had
never been out of the custody of their Toronto House.
On the other hand, Mr. Wells' book was written in

England, and he had not been in Canada when Miss Deeks' manuscript was in the custody of their Toronto House.

Miss Deeks took her case to an Associate Professor of Ancient and Old Testament Languages and Literature—the Rev. W. A. Irwin, M.A., D.B., Ph.D., at that time of Toronto University, afterwards, Professor of Old Testament Languages and Literature at Chicago University. This professor's own statement, as filed in Court, after telling of Miss Deeks' visit, and her request that he should undertake a study of the two works for evidence bearing upon her contention, goes on to say: "I consented in considerable measure because this is the sort of task with which my study of ancient literatures repeatedly confronts me, and I was interested to test out in modern works the methods commonly applied to those of the ancient world."

The subsequent history of this case ran as follows:

"Both the Ontario Court Judge, and the Ontario Court of Appeal Judges, completely rejected the evidence of the Higher Criticism, and dismissed the case. So Miss Deeks went to the Judicial Committee of the Privy Council in London, the highest legal Tribunal in the Empire. After a long hearing in which the Higher Criticism was again thoroughly reviewed, on 3rd November 1932, the Court unanimously dismissed the appeal."

The following are extracts from Lord Atkin's judgment as affecting the Higher Criticism part of the case:

"Miss Deeks relied in the Courts below upon the evidence of three literary gentlemen of considerable reputation who were entitled to be treated as experts on this subject. They pointed out coincidences, similarities, identical omissions, and so forth, which in their view led to the inference that one work was the copy of the other. Their Lordships have read that evidence and they notice that the expert witnesses were allowed in the Court below to give evidence as to the result of their opinions, and as to the effect of them, which appeared to their Lordships, not to be within the domain of expert evidence at all. The witnesses were apparently permitted to say not only that there were similarities, but that in their opinion the result of the similarities was such that in fact Mr. Wells did copy from this work—which of course is not a matter for expert testimony at all—and, indeed, one witness was permitted to give evidence to the effect that in his opinion Mr. Wells wrote his own book with the manuscript of Miss Deeks' book upon the desk before him, evidence which quite plainly was not a matter for expert opinion. . . .

"The suggested similarities can be explained by the nature of the work, which has common elements, and by the fact that both writers must have had recourse to authorities which were common to both. After all, neither Miss Deeks nor Mr. Wells was present at the beginning of the world or until a very considerable time later, and they have had to rely upon the accumulation of information which has been made by many authors before them and to which they have had to have recourse in writing such a work as this.

"Their Lordships do not pause to deal with the details of the evidence that was given, but in a great many cases it is quite properly described by one of the Judges as fantastic, and such actual coincidences as do exist are quite explicable, and should be explained in the manner suggested."

Such then has been the judicial attitude to Literary Criticism when applied to modern literature.

When we come to examine this Higher Criticism on its historical side, we are confronted with the disquieting fact that those standards of human knowledge, by which the Old Testament has been criticized and measured, are not themselves stable or constant, but ever changing. How was it possible to construct a system of Historical Criticism that would remotely represent Reality, by using the shifting sands of human knowledge of Ancient History? Until knowledge of remote ages of civilization became far more complete, it should have seemed obvious to any judicially minded critic, that History, as recorded in the Old Testament, was on the whole much more likely to be correct, than the meagre history available from other sources.

Nearly a century after Bible criticism had started, archæologists first began to dig in the mounds of ancient ruins in Bible lands, in order to increase existing knowledge of ancient history. So the sources of information were no longer derived from classical writers, combined with conjecture of what ought to have happened; but began to be slowly enriched by evidence left behind by those who lived in times that were mythical to Herodotus, and other ancient historians. During the last ten years, evidence from these far earlier sources has been piling in upon us, and in order to judge this evidence rightly, and assign it to its proper place, it must first be used to rectify existing historical standards. The defective character of these latter will soon be manifest; and since some at least are false, the historical conclusions based on them seem even more unsound than were the literary ones. *So it has become necessary to scrap most, if not all, of what people have learned or read about the Old Testament, in colleges and seminaries, in text-books, commentaries and encyclopædias, and to go back to the original books of Genesis, Exodus, Leviticus, Numbers, Deuteronomy and Joshua.*

In order to justify such a drastic rejection of erudition, the following are some specific examples of fundamental errors— that is to say, of mistakes which nullify the whole course of reasoning, and conclusions, of some particular critic, or group of critics.

There is no longer any doubt that the races who inhabited the Euphrates valley, Syria, Palestine, and Egypt, in ancient times, possessed a much higher culture than has been postulated for them by Bible critics. For example, we now know that the art of writing in cuneiform on clay tablets was in general use long before the days of Abraham. Archæological evidence has now established the fact that alphabetical writing was actually in existence in Sinai at the very time when Moses led the tribes there after the Exodus from Egypt; and further, that such writing was being used in Palestine immediately after the days of Moses. *It would almost seem as though civilized man has always had*

*the means for recording in writing, and did record in writing—
events, laws, customs, rituals, history, etc., everything such as
we find recorded in the books of Genesis, Exodus, etc.*

How different must have been the whole course of
criticism of the Old Testament had this evidence been
originally available and its significance appreciated a
century and a half ago! Critics have recently endeav-
oured to represent that they take into account the
fact of the art of writing being in existence in ancient
times. In this respect they only echo the words of the
late Canon S. R. Driver, one of the most celebrated of
the last generation of scholars. His dissections of the
first six books of the Old Testament led him to make the
following statement:

"The two earliest narratives are undoubtedly those
by J and E; these are based upon the oral traditions
current in the eighth and ninth centuries."

*So statements that purported to be made by Moses five
or six centuries earlier, were oral traditions of the eighth and
ninth centuries; and, in order to complete the critical diagnosis
of dates, were first committed to writing about 621 B.C.*

Now the pronouncements of distinguished professors
in every branch of learning, however positive they
may be, are nevertheless not immune from those canons
of common sense which control the conclusions of
ordinary mortals. So we are entitled to ask, how is it
possible for Canon Driver and his followers to postulate
oral traditions in the eighth or ninth centuries, if the
art of writing was in common use from before the days
of Moses and onwards?

When Driver goes on to affirm that he has taken account of the fact of the art of writing being in existence in ancient times, it can be pointed out in justice to his memory, that the statement was made before many of the archæological discoveries to which attention is about to be drawn in these pages.

But nevertheless, even in Canon Driver's day, it had become evident that all sorts of writing, certainly in cuneiform and hieroglyphic, were in common use in Syria and Palestine at the very time of Moses. His affirmation that he had taken account of the existence of such writing in framing his conclusion, is quoted by his followers to-day as though it were sufficient to override the effects of recent discoveries. It is unfortunate that Driver appears to have contented himself with a simple affirmation that the discovery of writing made no difference. For such a statement, even from Driver, imposes altogether too great a strain upon our credulity. It is as though someone were now to affirm that although handwriting was practised in Norman times and, moreover, was superseded by the printing press, yet nevertheless the account of the Norman conquest of England only existed in the form of oral tradition at the time of the restoration of the monarchy under Charles II. And that these oral traditions were first committed to writing in the early days of Queen Victoria! What would our readers think of such an assertion? So much for the ancient art of writing—oral tradition may be the method of transmission of the primitive peoples of the world, but the archæological evidence to be advanced in these pages *will prove that Abraham and his descendants cannot be placed in any such category.* It has been a blunder of the first order to suppose that they were anything of the sort.

Our next specific example of fundamental mistakes in Old Testament criticism is due to the attempt of commentators to apply the theory of evolution to religion. It is no part of this work to discuss the subject of evolution as applied to the physical side of humanity. But the attempt to apply evolution to the religious side is responsible for another long train of blunders in connection with the Bible. The following are examples from the works of distinguished and well-known contemporary writers:

"We have seen that religious belief in its gradual development among early races passed through the stages of Animism and Polytheism. Since this is recognized as a universal rule among all peoples whose religion develops sufficiently, we may assume that the Hebrews or their forbears were no exception."

The evidence of Anthropology will be cited in these columns to prove that the original religion of the "early races" was actually Monotheism or something very like it. So far as the Hebrews are concerned, or rather their forbears, the Semites, it is not necessary to "assume" anything, since the evidence of the ancient cuneiform writing, which will be referred to later, testifies to the fact that Monotheism was also their original religion.

Or to take another illustration:

"There was no heaven in the Semitic or Sumerian beliefs."

This strange statement appears also to be another evolutionary conjecture; and again the evidence of the cuneiform tablets indicates the belief, both of a heaven for the righteous, and the presence there of the bread of life and the water of life, which figure prominently some thousands of years later in the discourses of Jesus Christ.

A fourth example of fundamental mistakes in certain Bible commentaries, crops up in connection with the date of the Exodus. On inconclusive evidence it has long been assumed that the Exodus of the Israelites from Egypt took place in the reign of a Pharaoh named Mernepthah, about the year 1220 B.C. And because there was evidence, from Egyptian records, that the tribe of Asher was in its proper place in Palestine as early as 1300 B.C., elaborate theories have been evolved that most of the twelve tribes of Israel never went down into Egypt at all!

It would seem as though critics might have sensed the fact that the presence of the tribe of Asher in its proper place in Palestine, as early as 1300 B.C., presupposed an earlier date for the Exodus! Such an assumption was of a simpler character than to discredit the ancient narrative; but Bible commentators have rarely displayed any respect for the Old Testament when it stood in the way of their conjectures. Convincing evidence will be advanced in these columns to prove that the Exodus from Egypt occurred about the year 1440 B.C., or fully two hundred and twenty years earlier than the generally accepted date. There accordingly seems every reason why the tribe of Asher should have been in its proper place in Palestine before the year 1300 B.C.

Again: the views of authorities on the Old Testament narrative have been deflected by the speculations of German critics on the subject of the length of rule over Egypt of the Hyksos or Shepherd Kings. Instead of accepting the statements of the Egyptian historian Manetho that this mysterious race ruled over Egypt for over five centuries, the modern German critic has reduced this period to a century. Sir Flinders Petrie, who has spent years in excavating Hyksos sites, has come definitely to the conclusion that the reign of these Shepherd Kings lasted for an even longer period of time than is specified by Manetho.

And this brings us to yet another misunderstanding which seems to have arisen through disregarding the very definite statements made in the ninth chapter of Genesis. Critical works on the Bible are full of allusions to "Canaanite" civilization. Some German critics at least have thrown the Bible's genealogy of Abraham in Genesis xi. to the winds, and boldly affirmed that he was a Canaanite! But in Genesis ix. there is a curse placed upon Canaan; and upon his race, the Amorites, etc.

Attention will later be drawn to the fact that the

very word "Amurru," or Amorites, was used as a class name for labourers on the cuneiform tablets. And yet the Hebrew language, and even the introduction of writing, has been ascribed to them!

Archæological evidence will be cited to prove that the Canaanites and Amorites, like the Egyptians, derived their civilization from foreigners; from Abraham's relatives the Semites, who conquered and occupied both Syria and Palestine some seven centuries before his time; and that they in turn were followed by their relatives the Hyksos or Shepherd Kings. Gaza was the base used for the invasion of Egypt, but the camps of these Shepherd Kings are studded all over Syria and Palestine. Sir Flinders Petrie's excavations of Gaza have revealed contemporary evidence of Semitic occupation from 3000 B.C. to 1500 B.C. Evidence will be advanced for the residence round the Dead Sea before Abraham's time, of Arabs, also a branch of the Semitic race. Their alphabetical cuneiform tablets recently found are written in Archaic Hebrew, and dated 1400–1350 B.C. No doubt during the long occupation of both Syria and Palestine the Semites intermarried and became absorbed into the Canaanites and the Amorites. But to assume that the higher civilization and culture was brought by these inferior races, and learnt from them by Abraham and his descendants, is, to use a homely phraseology, putting the cart before the horse.

Those of our readers who remember what they have learned or read about the earlier books of the Old

Testament in recent years, those who are acquainted with even recent works on Biblical archæology, will appreciate the far-reaching effects of the new evidence that has come to light.

The most hardened critic may dispute some of these findings, but he must be a veritable fanatic who will entirely reject them; not at all the type of man postulated by the *Encyclopædia Britannica's* article for the position of a higher critic! And yet, those who are familiar with the historical criticism, can judge the effect of any or all of the following:

1. The evidence for the use of writing, including alphabetical writing, both before and after Moses, now supplied by archæology, makes conjectures about oral transmission unworthy of any further credit.

2. The theory of the evolution of Religion is contradicted by the evidence of both Archæology and Anthropology.

3. So is the assumption that ancient races, least of all Abraham's race, lacked any belief in a future life.

4. All that has been written or taught on the basis of the Exodus having taken place in 1220 B.C. proves also to be on an unsound foundation.

5. The emphasis laid on Canaanite culture is also based on unsound methods of interpretation.

These are only some of the historical mistakes on which the historical criticism has been reared, and the worst of it is, that those who have accepted one or more of them, are influenced to look with jaundiced eyes on the real significance of the archæological evidence.

To sum up then, whether we reflect upon the fate of the literary criticism in the Law Courts; or the historical criticism in the light of the new knowledge archæology is contributing to History; both these two components that together make up Higher Criticism, are seen to be unreliable, and their conclusions of no account. This justifies the invitation to neglect them for the traditional road mapped out by the Old Testament, and to endeavour to verify the route by studying the ancient landmarks that have been found.

The alternative of following the guidance and authority of critics and commentators in the light of recent knowledge, can but bewilder the issue and lead us all astray. It is quite obvious that the complete assurance, with which many wrote, has been entirely unjustified, even as it is discordant to the scientific outlook of the present day. Yet the mass of people are not aware of this fact; indeed many well-informed Christians have thought that the Higher Criticism, since it was endorsed and advocated, even by distinguished bishops, could be taken for granted as giving correct results. The effects of such grave errors upon Christianity in general, and the Church of England in particular, has been devastating.

The vast archæological discoveries of the past eight years resemble the fragments of some immense jig-saw puzzle; they need a guide to fit them together. The Old Testament has proved an excellent guide to the geography of the Holy Land; why should it not be a correct guide, in as far as it goes, to ancient History?

Such are the considerations with which readers are now invited to study the archæological evidence. It will be seen that much of it is the product of the last few years' work, that it is still quite incomplete; that more is needed. Many of our judgments must be tentative. We may not emulate the obtrusive confidence of Higher Critics. A superficial glance through the Old Testament reveals much on which Archæology has not yet borne any witness. We know nothing of David, and next to nothing of Solomon. So more digging is needed, especially in Palestine; more scholars to decipher the ancient writings. And on what better mission can men pour out money in these doubting days? But we do now know enough to enable us to clear the ground of error, and to get a good general direction.

Yet it should here be remarked that the Old Testament narrative sometimes makes contact with a country which has been even less explored than Palestine, or Egypt, or Syria—it is the region of space, the realm of the Unseen. The radio messages traverse such territory, so we are sufficiently familiar with it to accept what Science says of its reality. What are its secrets? Has it inhabitants? Whence come those messages and manifestations to which all ages of man, civilized as well as uncivilized, Christian as well as Pagan, bear witness? Men are still trying to weigh and measure the Bible by imperfect historical evidence, and by materialistic conceptions of the Unseen, which Science has now completely discarded.

III

ANCIENT ETHNOLOGY AND GEOGRAPHY

IT is astonishing what an amount of time and trouble learned men seem to have spent in order to put together an intelligible story of the early Origin of Races.

There appear to have arisen unaccountable objections to the information given in Genesis ix. and x., although for lack of knowledge it would have been much safer to have taken the narrative as it stood rather than trust to conjecture. But the critical intoxication seems to have dulled the sense of perspective, and there was no appreciation, until the flood deposits were found, that the Deluge was something more than myth and legend. Even to-day as one reads the correspondence in *The Times* on the subject of the Aryan race, one is struck by the absence of reference to the Bible narrative. The chapter which deals with the Bible account of the Dispersion will contain more detailed reference to this subject. In the meantime, at the dawn of history so far as we can learn from archæology at present, we seem to find evidence of a movement of civilization from the direction of the Caucasus, down through Palestine to Egypt. It will be read in the concluding chapter of this book that Mr. Starkey places the earliest civilization he has come across at Tell Duweir (Lachish) in South Palestine, as far back as 4000 B.C., and he goes on to say that the settlement there then, was more extensive than at any later time in the history of the place.

It will also be seen that Sir Flinders Petrie assigns a date of 3000 B.C. for the first great Palace at Old Gaza; and Professor Garstang attributes the earliest occupation of Jericho to 2500 B.C. Some of these dates will probably have to be adjusted; still it does appear to-day as though the earliest civilization of Egypt owed its origin to people who came through Palestine, and the date of Menes, the first Pharaoh of the First Dynasty of Egypt, is placed by Petrie at 4326 B.C (*Ancient Egypt: A Revision of History*).

So much then for the earliest civilization of Palestine proper; in this chapter let us concern ourselves with the nations who were there when the Israelites entered the land (1400 B.C.). But we must first take a glance at the geography of the country. The Palestine campaign was one of the leading features of the Great War; and it was perhaps the one of which Britain has most reason to be proud. The splendid generalship contrasted with much ineffectual leadership on other fronts. Experience gained in this campaign led our soldiers to appreciate what an excellent guide to the geography of the country is found in the Old Testament. So the geography of the Bible narrative may be relied on as being correct. Archæology, on the other hand, is teaching us that the impressions we acquired as children about the nature and size of Canaan and its cities are not so accurate. This is scarcely, however, the fault of the Bible. Travellers who have visited Canaan have been heard to scoff at the idea of its being described as "a land flowing with milk and honey." But they are usually people who lack imagination, and fail to take account of the lapse of time, the changes of cilmate, and the ravages of endless wars and misrule. The barren rocky slopes that confront us to-day, carry traces of once having been covered with vines and olive-trees; with oaks and acacias, with fig-trees and flowers. In the days when the rainfall was abundant and regular, there would be no lack of food for the bees, or fodder for the flocks and herds.

The whole country is, however, only about the size of Wales, less than one hundred and fifty miles in length, from Dan in the north, to Beersheba in the south, and to-day some of its scenery recalls the wildest parts of Wales. The position of Palestine in a map of the world accords with the place assigned to it in as yet unfulfilled Bible prophecies. It is not difficult to picture its importance when peace and good government make effective the marvellous strides of modern civilization. Europe and Asia have given a taste of their possibilities in past history. But what of the whole of that huge continent of Africa, which, with the exception of Egypt and the Mediterranean coast, has never yet been developed? And the land link or meeting-ground of all these three great continents is the little country of Palestine.

Instead, however, of picturing its future, we must hark back to its remote past. In the days when the Israelites under Joshua entered their Promised Land, there existed the splendid civilization of Egypt to the south. The wealth of treasure found in the tomb of Tutankhamen, a Pharaoh almost contemporary with Joshua, is archæology's evidence for the correctness of this statement. To the north was the land of Syria with its coastlands, and here too was an advanced contemporary civilization, ample testimony to which has been unearthed at Ras Shamra. Beyond Syria was the great Hittite empire, while branching away eastwards were the vast civilizations of Mesopotamia.

These countries were all connected by trade routes, and Canaan connected them all with Egypt. Yet the hilly and rocky character of the interior of Canaan exempted much of the country from these comings and goings of foreigners. Whether for war, or for peace, the great highway through the country ran along what might be called "the Coastland Corridor." This corridor consists of a strip of land about one hundred miles long and fifteen miles wide, which runs due north from Gaza, parallel with the Mediterranean, and terminates in the great mass of Mount Carmel. All along this corridor the land is comparatively flat and highly fertile. It constitutes an ideal passage-way for armies, particularly for armies allied with sea power.

The country that runs parallel with this coastland corridor, and so lies between it and the Jordan valley, is about thirty miles wide, and constitutes the highlands.

It was among these hills and mountains that the tribes of Israel settled after the conquest by Joshua, all except the tribes of Reuben, Gad and half of Manasseh, who recrossed the Jordan and occupied the land on the east side in what is now Transjordania. This has been a less known and less explored region of the country, both by tourists and archæologists. It is a land of ascents and descents, of high hills and deep valleys, at the bottom of which run streams that flow into the Jordan. This country borders on the desert, and along its border ran an important trade route to which reference will be made at the end of this chapter.

This brief outline of the Promised Land is incomplete without reference to the great plain of Esdraelon in the north, which begins between the modern town of Haifa and the ancient city of Acre, both on the coast, and passes round Carmel and its neighbouring hills. It keeps south and east till it almost reaches the great descent into the Jordan valley. East of Carmel it is encircled by more highlands and by Mount Tabor, to the north-east of which is the Lake of Galilee.

The interior of Palestine has one peculiar feature most marked and most impressive, which, while it enters into the background of Bible history, is quite often unappreciated by the vast number of Bible readers who have not visited the country. Nevertheless this formation is closely connected with prophecies of the future. We refer to the great rift cutting through the country from north to south, and to the fact that the bottom of this rift runs a long way below the sea-level

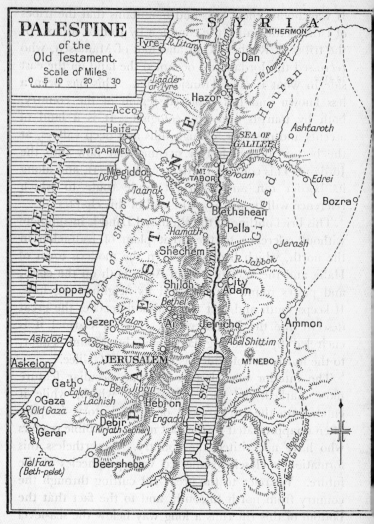

of the Mediterranean. The rift begins above the Lake of Galilee. There must be many readers of the New Testament who fail to realize that this sheet of water, on whose shores so much of Christ's work was done, is itself no less than seven hundred feet below the level of the Mediterranean. Thence the Jordan flows down through the rift for sixty-five miles, until it enters the north end of the Dead Sea. And the Dead Sea itself, with the adjacent plain of the Jordan on which Jericho stands, is thirteen hundred feet below the Mediterranean. In contrast to this deep depression, little more than thirty miles west of it, in the direction of the Mediterranean, stands Jerusalem, no less than twenty-four hundred feet above sea-level, surrounded by other hills of varying heights. The prophecies of the future, to which reference has just been made, predict a day when the Mount of Olives shall split in sunder (Zech. xiv. 4, Ezek. xlvii. 8), and water will pour into the great rift and presumably fill it up.

It is interesting to note that the earthquake, which shook Palestine in 1927, cracked the Mount of Olives.

The renowned General Gordon in 1883, immediately before he was sent to Khartoum to rescue the Soudan from the Mahdi, visited Palestine. Well acquainted as he was with the difficulties of holding the Suez Canal, he formulated a scheme for cutting a canal from Haifa to the Jordan, across the Plain of Esdraelon, and so filling the rift from the Mediterranean. Thus the water level of the Dead Sea would be raised 1300 feet. Then in order to gain access to the Red Sea and Indian

Ocean, he proposed to cut a further channel at the south end of the Dead Sea, through the intervening barrier of hills to the Gulf of Akaba. He estimated that the cost of the work in his day would be about twelve million pounds.

Those who are acquainted with the Palestine campaign of Lord Allenby in the Great War will remember how his army entered the country from Egypt; and how Gaza on the west, and Jericho on the east, became bases from which the invasion of the country was made. In reading the following chapters it will be noticed that the Gaza route was the one traversed by the ancient Egyptian armies in the course of their various invasions of Syria. Conversely down that coastland corridor from the north came Egypt's invaders. As already pointed out, this route's proximity to the Mediterranean offered great advantages to whoever possessed control of the sea, and this fact probably had an important bearing upon some of the operations.

Let us glance again at some of those nations to the north of Palestine who certainly used this coastland corridor with advantage ages before and after Joshua.

For two hundred miles the coast of Syria was peopled by the Phœnicians, concerning whom a good deal will be found in these pages. Long before the time of Joshua these people had become a great sea-faring race. How they must have used that ancient seaport of Old Gaza which Sir Flinders Petrie is now excavating! The Phœnicians, so their records suggest, were originally responsible for the nautical activity of the Greeks and other dwellers in the coastlands and islands of the Mediterranean. One of their protégés appear to have been the Philistines, or Pulasati, those armour-clad warriors that figure so prominently in the Books of Judges and Samuel, and whose penetration and power caused the land of Canaan to be called Palestine.

To the north, beyond Syria, was the great empire of the Hittites. It has been suggested that these people were of European origin, and connect up with the Trojans of Homer. Other northern races are now being identified with the aid of the ancient remains. Among them the Hurrians, a Caucasian race, now identified with the Bible Horites. A branch of these were the people of Mitanni who, about the time of Joshua, were ruled by an Indo-European dynasty. Their deities appear to have been Indra, Varuna, and Mitra. They seem to constitute the Aryan link with India and Europe in ancient times.

In the tenth chapter of Genesis there is a description of the sons of Noah and their descendants. It appears to be a document of extreme antiquity, and represents the original dispersions of the sons of Noah. Speaking roughly we judge that Shem's descendants were originally settled in Asia and Arabia, Ham's in Asia Minor and Africa, and Japheth's in Europe. Thus, from this ancient aspect, Canaan became the meeting-ground of all the descendants of Noah—a fit stage, indeed, for the greatest drama of humanity.

Beside the coastland corridor on the west of Palestine, an important trade-route ran along the eastern border

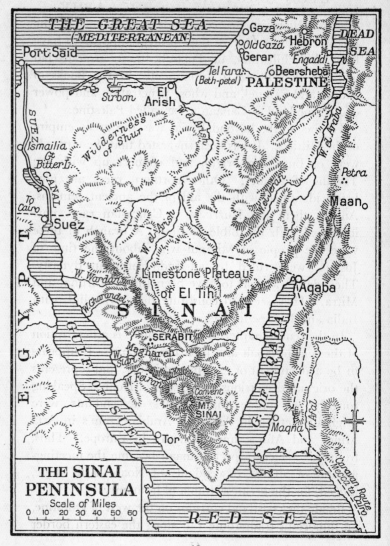

THE GREAT SEA
(MEDITERRANEAN)

Port Said

Gaza
Old Gaza
Gerar

Hebron

DEAD
SEA

Tel Fara
(Beth-petel)

Engaddi

Beersheba

PALESTINE

L.
Sirbon

El
Arish

W. Arish

Ismailia
Gt.
Bitter L.

SUEZ

Wilderness
of Shur

W. el Araba

To
Cairo

CANAL

Petra

Maan

Suez

W. el Arish

Limestone Plateau

W. Wardan

of El Tih

Aqaba

W. Gharandel

SINAI

SERABIT

EGYPT

W. Maghareh
W. Sidri

GULF OF SUEZ

W. Faran

Convent
MT.
SINAI

G. OF AQABA

W. Afal

Tor

Maqna

Caravan Route
Mecca to Cairo

THE SINAI
PENINSULA

Scale of Miles

0 10 20 30 40 50 60

RED   SEA

42

of the land from remote time. This caravan road came down from Damascus in the north, and ran due south through the Hauran: it passed some distance east of the Dead Sea, and continued south past Mount Seir to the Gulf of Akaba on the Red Sea.

Here let our readers refresh their memory with a glance at our map of the Sinai Peninsula. They will notice that the north end of the Red Sea ends in two arms or gulfs—the western one being the Gulf of Suez, which the Suez Canal now connects with the Mediterranean; the eastern one is the Gulf of Akaba to which reference has just been made. Incidentally, it should be noted that between these two gulfs is the Sinai Peninsula, in the centre of which rises the sacred mountain of Sinai, the traditional spot whence the Law was delivered unto Moses.

Opposite the Peninsula of Sinai, on the eastern shore of the Gulf of Akaba, is the country of Midian, to which Moses fled for refuge when he was about forty years old. More will be said about Midian in connection with the life of Moses. Meantime let it be noted that it is bounded on the north by Lat. 29° 29′ and on the south by Lat. 27° 39′. In other words it extends from the head of the Gulf of Akaba, and down the eastern shore of the Red Sea for about two hundred miles in all. It did not, however, include the Peninsula of Sinai. To-day it forms part of the Hedjaz of Arabia.

For many years the author's endeavours have been made to glean further information regarding this district; but the region is little known, and still rather inaccessible. It seems likely that a motor road will shortly be completed from Egypt to Akaba, but in the spring of 1933 it was not ready for use. And the exploration of the eastern shore of the Gulf appeared to be impracticable.

Information about this coast is becoming important for a correct understanding of the early Old Testament background. The legendary site of Ophir is laid either in South Arabia, or even in Africa, and there is little doubt that in the days of King Solomon, the precious metal was brought up the Red Sea to the head of the Gulf, known in the Old Testament as Ezion-geber. At an even earlier date Ezion-geber is mentioned in connection with the wanderings of the children of Israel in the Wilderness.

Thus the trade-route from Damascus to the Red Sea, and so to the Indian Ocean, along the borders of Eastern Palestine, was always of great importance. Where this road passes through the Hauran, are the remains of cities that flourished in the period 2500–1600 B.C.

Before concluding this chapter a further reference should be made to the great rift or Jordan valley. In places it is still somewhat inaccessible and, at any rate, on its eastern site it needs further examination and exploration. But it is said to be plagued with mosquitoes, and malaria is prevalent. Some commentators have assumed that its barren soil and sultry atmosphere have always existed in this deep canyon; but recent examinations testify to the fact that it was once a most fertile part of the country.

The cataclysm which overwhelmed Sodom and Gomorrah and the other cities of the plain, now perhaps submerged beneath the waters of the Dead Sea, seems to have changed the climate, at any rate, at the lower end of the valley. So Jericho, though a delightful place in winter, becomes unendurably hot in summer; and similar climatic conditions, together with the mosquitoes, prevail higher up the Jordan.

During recent years, however, the distinguished American archæologist, Dr. W. F. Albright, has explored the district, and found ample evidence that the most prosperous period of the rift was before 2000 B.C. The new Bible chronology which will be set down later on in this book, indicates that the destruction of Sodom and Gomorrah occurred about 2061 B.C. The significance of Dr. Albright's discovery will be appreciated when the stories of the life of Abraham are discussed.

The author has recently been interested in some research work at Pella, in the Jordan valley, where there are remains going back to great antiquity. A reference to this spot in connection with Joshua will be made later in this work, but it is really chiefly interesting from its primitive Christian settlement. It was to Pella that the early Christians fled for refuge when Titus and his Romans besieged Jerusalem in A.D. 70. In this remote spot, protected by all manner of rock shelters, caves, and subterranean passages, as yet unexplored, they were saved from the slaughter which attended the destruction of Jerusalem.

IV

THE NATURE OF THE EVIDENCE

HISTORY tells us that the Romans conquered England, and added it to their Empire some forty or fifty years after Christ. In various parts of our country, usually about two feet below the surface, are the remains of four centuries of Roman civilization to testify to the correctness of this history.

In like manner beneath the surface of the soil, in Palestine and Syria, in Mesopotamia and Egypt, are ample remains of a far older civilization to testify to the correctness of Old Testament history.

Viewed as a whole, the evidence is extraordinarily impressive. When details are examined, it is more difficult, because account must be taken of the incompleteness of our knowledge. The failure to observe this precaution has proved to be a grave defect in many modern Bible commentaries. If there had been no evidence of early Bible civilization, such, for example, as that outlined in the Book of Genesis, there might have been justification. But our readers will soon note that there is any amount of evidence. What the Romans left behind them in England, seems trifling to what those who lived in the days of Abraham have left behind them in Mesopotamia. In England, there are a few Latin inscriptions on tombstones, or of a dedicatory character from the ruins of public buildings, or on ancient milestones, and that is about all the writing left by the Romans in Britain.

But in Mesopotamia, Asia Minor, Egypt, Syria, and Persia, excavators have been finding whole libraries of clay tablets, covered with writing, in the cuneiform or wedge-shaped characters, and in other scripts; and there must be plenty more still beneath the soil. For the present, the problem appears to be rather more a matter of decipherment, dating, classification, and interpretation, of the quantities of clay documents already found, than looking for more of them. But there are far too few scholars for this class of work. If the time wasted on minute dissection of the Bible text—on straining at gnats and swallowing camels —had been spent in learning to read cuneiform tablets, there would be a far clearer knowledge of ancient history to-day than at present is the case. But the discernment, skill, patience and perseverance required for this kind of work, render this form of scholarship a far from popular one, at any rate in England. So decipherers are few, and we are forced to depend much on German scholarship. Without wishing to deprecate the fine work of other countries in this important branch of research, it is essential that more attention should be given to it in the universities of England and America. What is the use of teaching students an ancient history of the world, still largely based on conjecture and the classics, when there are in existence original contemporary documents to tell us what the people of Abraham's day studied, or the people of Moses' time believed; what were their customs; how they bought and sold; what laws their rulers made, how long they reigned, and what they did?

For the purposes of this book it is only necessary to enumerate some of the sources of information of this character, such as the cuneiform tablets found in Mesopotamia—at Nippur, by the University of Pennsylvania's Expeditions; or at Kish and Jemdet Nasr by Dr. Langdon, with the aid of the Field Museum at Chicago; or at Boghazkoi by the Germans; or at Ras Shamra in Syria by Messrs. Schaefer and Chenet.

Let us also recall the fact that as long ago as A.D. 1887, a group of cuneiform tablets was found among the ruins of Tel el Amarna, in Egypt. These had been written by the petty Kings of Syria and Palestine between 1400–1360 B.C. and sent to two Pharaohs, whose reigns cover this period. These letters acquire new importance in the light of the evidence from the Jericho excavations recorded later.

Then in 1906–7, Dr. Winckler found a royal Hittite library at Boghaz Keui, in Asia Minor, about one hundred and fifty miles inland south of Sinope, a port on the south shore of the Black Sea. This collection of cuneiform and other tablets, when discovered, appear to have been beautifully arranged in pigeon-holes, and classified. The tablets were removed to Berlin, and it was only after the commencement of the Great War that Dr. F. Hrozny discovered that the language in which some of them were written was related to the Indo-European group. The task of deciphering and correlating these tablets is still going on, and their publication will obviously modify and affect present knowledge.

There are frequent references to these Hittites in the Old Testament, and although this race belonged to the northern part of Asia Minor, yet Abraham purchased the cave of Machpelah as a burial-place from a Hittite family, and Machpelah is close to Hebron in Southern Palestine. Again: the prophet Ezekiel, inveighing against the wickedness of Jerusalem in his day, reminds the city that it was founded by Amorites and Hittites—a further testimony to the presence of the latter in Southern Palestine, even before the days of Abraham.

As far back as 1905, Sir Flinders Petrie undertook an expedition into the Peninsula of Sinai, the traditional scene of the wanderings of the Israelites under Moses. On the top of one of its mountains he explored the ruins of a Semitic temple, of which more will be written in a later chapter. The purpose of this allusion is to direct attention to the fact that here Sir Flinders discovered the earliest alphabetical writing yet known. Much of it had been destroyed by gross acts of vandalism; and the decipherment of the fragments that remain has been a slow and precarious task for scholars. A recent publication assigned a date of about 1850–1800 B.C. to these writings; and they have now been linked up with the ancient Phœnician script, the ancestor of our own, by the inscription on the ewer from Tell Duweir (see frontispiece).

Some three years ago, the excavation of a mound on the coast of Northern Syria, opposite the island of Cyprus, led to a discovery of immense importance. The mound proved to contain the ruins of a temple, in the basement of which a small library of inscribed clay tablets were brought to light. The place where this treasure trove was discovered is called Ras Shamra. Some of the tablets were written in the cuneiform script, some in conventional Babylonian, others in the Sumerian or priestly language. But more important still, were others, written in a script which consisted of only twenty-seven different characters, as compared with the several hundred involved combinations of the older Babylonian syllabary. It was obvious that the ancient cuneiform writing-signs had been used for the purpose of recording an alphabetical script; and the fact that the characters were twenty-seven in number suggested a language of twenty-seven letters. The problem was how to decipher it.

In Edgar Allan Poe's story, *The Gold Bug*, there is a description of the decipherment of a cryptogram. In more recent years, Conan Doyle, the creator of the Sherlock Holmes detective stories, made his hero solve the cryptogram of *The Dancing Men*, by employing methods similar to those described in Poe's story. Now the alphabetical cuneiform writing found at Ras Shamra was really nothing more nor less than a cryptogram; and by using Poe's method, Professor Bauer, of Halle, discovered which letters of the alphabet were represented by each of the twenty-seven different characters.

The language proved to be archaic Hebrew; and the date of the tablets has been provisionally fixed at 1400–1350 B.C. Only a portion of these tablets have yet been deciphered, so it is hazardous to base definite conclusions upon them. But it is already quite clear that they connect up with the worship of the Israelites in the Wilderness, as instituted by Moses. Frequent reference will be made to these Ras Shamra tablets in succeeding pages. On the other hand, the actual finds of cuneiform tablets, among the ruined sites of Palestine, have, up to the present, been few and far between; but allusions will be made in the pages that follow to isolated examples, which contain evidence of importance.

Our readers are doubtless aware that writing in Egypt in the form of hieroglyphics goes back to an extremely ancient time, and that scholars are well versed in this type of writing. Quantities of it exist which deal with all periods of Egyptian history, and much of it has been deciphered and published during the past fifty years. Sir Flinders Petrie has expressed the opinion that, in some respects, we know more about the Egyptian history of ancient times, than we do about Anglo-Saxon history during the period that followed England's evacuation by the Romans.

It is highly probable that, as the varieties of Bible

evidence, now revealed, come to be studied and correlated, and previous unsound assumptions and conclusions are consigned to the limbo of forgotten things, it may be found that both Joseph and Moses can be identified with characters already known in Egyptian history.

Another class of evidence, which is of great value, is that supplied through the excavation of the ruined sites themselves. Apart from the broken pottery and scarabs (which will be dealt with later), inscriptions are being sometimes found, and potsherds, on which are scraps of writing.

Once again: there is the evidence furnished by ancient walls, or the contents of the interior of tombs, temples, houses, and palaces. As will be seen, Ur of the Chaldees, Old Gaza, and Tell Duweir (Lachish), have yielded much valuable information in this respect. So did the excavations made outside Jerusalem in 1925-6-7 by the Palestine Exploration Fund, with which the author was associated. There was found the remains of the old Jebusite city of Jerusalem, with its wall twenty-four feet in thickness. But the place of honour belongs to Jericho, whose fallen walls, and burnt, but unplundered interior, gave remarkable confirmation to the Bible story of its capture and destruction.

And then there is yet another class of evidence of their own time left by those who lived when Abraham, Isaac, Jacob, Joseph, Moses, and Joshua walked the earth. It should be borne in mind that this new type of evidence—the evidence, that is, of the potsherds or broken pieces of earthenware—has really only been available during the past eight years. A tourist who visits the Holy Land, soon becomes aware of the fact that it is studded with the sites of small ruined cities; and they in turn, both above and below the present surface of the soil, are littered with fragments of pottery. They must have been great users and good breakers of pots, these ancient Amorites and Canaanites, and all the rest of them! And the Israelites, when they came upon the scene, did their share in this construction and destruction of earthenware.

In the course of several thousands of years of civilization, which the country has enjoyed, its little cities with their great outer walls of defence, have been destroyed and rebuilt again and again. Usually the same site has been chosen, and ruins of the previous occupation have been levelled and used for the foundation of the next city, and so on. Thus the excavator finds layer upon layer of pottery fragments, one underneath the other, each layer marking some fresh occupation and destruction.

The fashions in ancient earthenware were not so variable as modern ladies' hats and dresses, nevertheless, in the course of centuries there were developments and changes and importations from abroad. It was Sir Flinders Petrie who was the first to appreciate the possibilities of using the variations of pottery for chronological purposes. And to make a long story short, since the Great War these variations have been classified, and dates assigned to them. The dates have principally been obtained with the aid of Egyptian scarabs found among the layers of fragments. These scarabs, or seals, have inscribed upon them the names of Pharaohs whose dates are known. Since the year 1925, and largely through the excavation of Beth-Shan, or Beisan, a city in the north of Palestine, occupied as a strategic post by the Egyptians, from about 1480–1200 B.C., it has been considered possible to identify, and to date, the periods of occupation of a particular site, from the different layers of potsherds upon it. So the chronology and, to some extent, the history of a mound of ruins can be reconstructed; not, of course, without other evidence to a specific year, or two years, or even ten, but to, perhaps in certain instances, a quarter of a century.

Readers will be spared further technical details about ancient potsherds, except that the classes into which they have been divided and dated are as follows:

The Early Bronze Age . . . 2500–2000 B.C.
The Middle Bronze Age . . . 2000–1600 B.C.
The Late Bronze Age . . . 1600–1200 B.C.

At the time of writing it has become fairly obvious that the word "Copper" should be substituted for "Bronze," for the old metal weapons and implements found prove on analysis to be of pure copper. But to avoid confusion it still seems best to adhere to the old title. For purposes of comparison with the above, the dates of some Bible events for which evidence will be cited in later chapters, are as follows:

The Flood	Prior to 2500 B.C.
Abraham	2160–1985 B.C.
The Israelites' sojourn in Egypt .	1870–1440 B.C.
The Exodus, and the wandering in the Wilderness	1440–1400 B.C.
The Fall of Jericho	1400 B.C.
The Conquest of Canaan . .	1400–1360 B.C.
Period of the Judges . . .	1360–1018 B.C.
Reign of Saul, David and three years of Solomon	1018– 957 B.C.
Founding of Solomon's Temple .	957 B.C.

These dates are based upon the date of the Fall of Jericho, which Professor Garstang places at 1407 B.C., or seven years earlier. In like manner the founding of Solomon's Temple has been placed in 967 B.C. by some authorities. So a margin of ten years should be allowed. Thus the evidence cited places the Exodus between 1447–1437 B.C.

Other, and most important evidence, for dating purposes are the scarabs, which may be said to resemble the seals on finger rings. They emanate from Egypt, and are relics of Egyptian relations with Canaan, to which frequent references are made in the succeeding chapters. When the scarabs are found engraved with the cartouche of a Pharaoh, they give excellent indications of the date of a particular site, or of a particular strata of pottery. As will be seen, the scarabs discovered in Jericho's tombs have been an invaluable confirmation of the pottery system of dating.

55

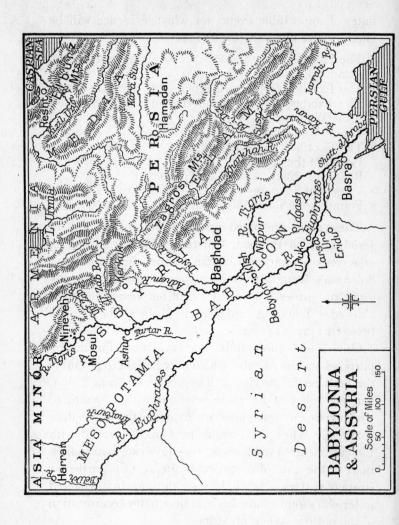

V

PRIMEVAL RELIGION AND THE TEN PATRIARCHS

THE scene of the events recorded in the earlier chapters of the Book of Genesis appears to be laid in the neighbourhood of the River Euphrates. The surrounding country is called the land of Shinar, or the land of the Chaldees, or Mesopotamia. We have known it as Babylonia; to-day, it is styled the kingdom of Iraq.

It is a land of alluvial plains or mud flats through which the Euphrates and Tigris flow down to the Persian Gulf. But the deserts are studded with the ruins of ancient cities, and seared with the channels of old irrigation canals; the sand has submerged all.

Beneath the surface, excavations reveal the remains of a vast civilization, reaching back more than five thousand years before the time of Christ. These evidences of an age, quite mythical to the classical writers, have been left by two great races—the Sumerians and the Semites. The latter take their name from Shem, the eldest son of Noah, and the Hebrew race, from which Abraham sprang, was a branch of this people.

The confident tone adopted by some modern writers

57

of ancient history, tends to create the impression that everything is already known about these very ancient times. That has been an entirely wrong conception. Every year during the last ten years some important discovery has been made; and there must be any amount of evidence which remains to be uncovered. As human knowledge is enlarged, the apparently assured facts of but a few years ago become the proven fiction of to-day.

It would appear to be quite insecure to embark upon confident conjectures. But what *does* emerge from this twilight-time of history is the fact that already its cuneiform clay tablets and pictures testify to the earlier chapters of the Book of Genesis. It may not be said that they furnish the irrefutable truth of these chapters; but they do suggest the probability that under different names, and in perhaps another theological setting, the children of Abraham's time were taught stories about the Creation, the Temptation, the Death of Abel, the Patriarchs before the Flood, and of the Deluge itself, such as children are taught to-day. Let us try to realize that none of these tales were invented during the last four thousand years.

But the outstanding feature of all this remote civilization in its relation to the Bible is the evidence it affords that Monotheism (the belief in one supreme God) preceded polytheism, or the belief in many gods. This is the very careful and deliberate conclusion of Dr. Langdon, Professor of Assyriology at Oxford, probably the greatest living authority on cuneiform literature, and this very remote period of civilization. It is a conclusion of such far-reaching consequence that there hardly seems to be a modern book written about the Old Testament, or about Ancient History, or about archæology in Bible lands, which remains unaffected by it.

It would seem as though nearly all modern writers on these subjects have been so hypnotized by the theory of evolution, that they have been led to place an entirely wrong emphasis on the evidence with which they have dealt; and, in some cases at least, to have misunderstood its significance altogether.

If Dr. Einstein's hypothesis of Relativity is true, it renders all previous books on Physics obsolete. In like manner Dr. Langdon's discovery that Monotheism was the original Religion, must have a similar effect on all books that refer to ancient faiths.

In view of the importance of this discovery, let us extract some brief references from Dr. Langdon's book *Semitic Mythology* (vol. v. in the series, *The Mythology of all Races*, published by the Archæological Institute of America, Marshall Jones Company, Boston, and used by permission). In his Introduction (p. xviii) Dr. Langdon writes:

"I may fail to carry conviction in concluding that, both in Sumerian and Semitic religions, monotheism preceded polytheism and belief in good and evil spirits. The evidence and reasons for this conclusion, so contrary to accepted and current views, have been set down with care and with the perception of adverse criticism. It is, I trust, the conclusion of knowledge and not of audacious preconception."

It will be remembered that in the opening chapter a modern writer is quoted as *assuming* that the Hebrew religion passed through a period of animism and polytheism before it arrived at monotheism. The following passage contradicts that theory:

"Although the South Arabians and Accadians are far advanced beyond the primitive Bedouin stage in the periods when the inscriptions begin, their history shows that it is characteristic of the Semites to use animal names in times of advanced culture, when there is no possible influence of primitive totemism. *I therefore reject the totemistic theory absolutely.* Early Canaanitish and Hebrew religions are far beyond primitive totemism (if it ever existed among them) in the period when any definite information can be obtained about them . . . all Semitic tribes appear to have started with a single tribal deity whom they regarded as the Divine Creator of his people " (p. 11).

Later Dr. Langdon writes:

"The Semitic word for God meant originally 'He who is High,' a sky god; and here also I believe that their religion began with monotheism; they probably worshipped El, Ilah, as their first Deity " (p. 93).

Since Dr. Langdon's book was written, the cuneiform alphabetical script tablets found at Ras Shamra on the coast of Syria, have supplied ample evidence that with all their polytheism, El was the supreme Deity, and particularly the supreme Deity of Canaan.

Elsewhere in this notable book, Dr. Langdon quotes the statement of Sanchuniathon, a Phœnician sage of about 1000 B.C., but quoting from far earlier sources, that the principal Deity of Gebal (Byblus) was Elioun, and that he was called Hypsistos—or Most High.

It is obvious that this Elioun is the same as "El Elyon" of Genesis xiv., translated "God Most High" in the Authorized Version. As a result of his excavations at Kish Dr. Langdon writes:

"In my opinion, the history of the oldest religion of man is a rapid decline from monotheism to extreme polytheism and wide-spread belief in evil spirits. It is in a very true sense the history of the fall of man" (*Field Museum Leaflet*, 28).

Such is a well-considered verdict derived from a study of this ancient Mesopotamian literature. And now the Ras Shamra tablets have come on the scene to suggest that Sanchuniathon's writings were genuine, and in other respects to endorse the correctness of Dr. Langdon's deductions.

It seems hardly necessary to remind our readers how well this religious atmosphere of the twilight of Ancient History accords with the narrative contained in the earlier chapters of the Book of Genesis.

Before the evolutionary theory of religion came to prejudice the evidence of religious beliefs derived from other ancient civilizations, there seems to have been a tendency to come to the same conclusion as that now reached by Dr. Langdon. Thus, Sir Peter Le Page Renouf, the translator of the *Egyptian Book of the Dead*, wrote:

"M. de Rouge then says that from, or rather before, the beginning of the historical period, the pure monotheistic religion passed through the phase of Sabeism. . . . It is therefore more than five thousand years since, in the valley of the Nile, the hymn began to the Unity of God and the immortality of the soul. . . . The belief in the Unity of the Supreme God and in HIS attributes as Creator and Lawgiver—these are the primitive notions enchased like indestructible diamonds in the midst of the mythological superfetations accumulated in the centuries."

Sir Peter's comment (*The Hibbert Lectures*, 1879) on this quotation is:

"It is incontestably true that the sublimer portions of the Egyptian religion are not the comparatively late result of a process of development or elimination from the grosser."

The ancient Chinese records also supply evidence of original monotheism. In other countries indications seem much the same. Thus the Greek dramatist Æschylus is reported to have said:

"Zeus is the ether, Zeus the earth, Zeus the heaven,
   Zeus is the Universe and what is beyond the Universe."

When we further notice how Zeus Pater is the same as the Dyaus-Petar of ancient India, the same as the Jupiter of the Latin nations, and the same as the Tyr of the old Norse, the implication is strong that these several races all once had the same "Heaven Father"; the same monotheistic Faith; which degenerated into polytheism, as in Mesopotamia, Egypt, and China.

And now in that very year of 1931 which witnessed the publication of Dr. Langdon's work, came another book containing similar conclusions from another science to that of Archæology.

The science of Anthropology and Comparative Religion, studies the manners, and customs, and superstitions, and beliefs of the primitive or aboriginal races of the world. We are indebted to its leading authority for *The Origin and Growth of Religion—Facts and Theories* (Methuen, 1931). The conclusion reached by the author—Professor Schmidt of Vienna—in that volume, are derived from evidence collected all over the world. They testify to a universal belief in one Supreme Being, and a universal belief in a future life among the primitive peoples.

On this subject of a future life, the Mesopotamian tablets have revealed another piece of evidence of equal significance and importance to Old Testament students. As a result of his decipherment of these cuneiform inscriptions Dr. Langdon has reached the further conclusion that:

"The theological view running through Babylonia before 2000 B.C. was of a Heaven for the righteous, whom the Gods might choose to receive into Paradise where is the Bread and Water of Eternal Life."

Before the time of Abraham then, *before* any book of the Old Testament was written, and right down through the centuries *after* every book in the Old Testament had been written, there existed this belief in a future life, and the presence of the bread and water of eternal life in heaven. The possession of this knowledge enhances the significance of Jesus Christ's statements in the New Testament:

"I am the Bread of Life." (John vi. 35.)

"I am the Living Bread which came down from Heaven; if any man eat of this Bread he shall live for ever." (John vi. 51.)

"The water that I shall give him shall become in him a well of water springing up unto everlasting life." (John iv. 14.)

It is impressive to think that these statements of Christ, which seem to-day mysterious to some, and which were regarded as mysterious to many of His hearers (John vi. 52 and 60), conveyed a reference to primeval religious beliefs.

Among the cuneiform tablets that have been found is one of a king who praises himself because he "loved to read the writings of the age before the Flood." There is ample evidence of the existence of such records; and it is said that the mystery religions, practised at least six or seven centuries before Christ, owed their origin to them. Indeed, as knowledge increases, it may prove that Christianity, although connected to the Jewish religion, was actually the fulfilment of far more ancient religions than the one instituted in the days of Moses.

One cannot leave this subject of primeval belief in a future life, testified to now by the two sciences of Archæology and Anthropology, without a single allusion

64

to the harm that has been done by those who valued the conjectures of evolution before the evidence of fact. Was it perchance due to such influences that Old Testament passages like the following were explained away?

"But as for me I know that my Redeemer liveth,
And at last he will stand upon the earth;
And after my skin hath been thus destroyed,
Yet from my flesh shall I see God."

(Job xix. 25; margin.)

There is evidence of the ten patriarchs, mentioned in the fifth chapter of Genesis, in some of the early classical writings. But with the hasty conclusions that have been in vogue, they have naturally been treated as myths and legends, and unworthy of serious attention. But the recently discovered clay prism in the Ashmolean Museum, Oxford, of which an illustration is given, contains long lists of succession of kings and their dates. It commences with the names of eight kings who reigned before the Flood. These correspond with the ten patriarchs mentioned in the fifth chapter of the Book of Genesis. It is now known that these ten patriarchs figure under various names, in the mythologies of other civilizations, such as the Sumerian, the Greek, the Phœnician, and the Indian, as well as the Hebrew. It is true that there are discrepancies, and these heroes are represented as having lived for much longer periods of time than is allowed them even in the Old Testament narrative. But when all is said and done, the fact of their being mentioned from so many independent sources, some of which are extremely ancient, suggests that they must have had some sort of existence.

Reference has just been made to the writings before the Flood. It seems quite possible that some of these have survived, and may yet be deciphered and published. Later cuneiform sources represent them as relating to divination, to medicine and to mystic rituals of expiation or sacrifice. In Chapter XVI some further reference will be made to this subject. In the meantime, let us pass to the more definite evidence for the existence of the Flood.

VI

THE DELUGE AND THE DISPERSION

IT is only six years ago since it seemed improbable that a background of reality would ever be recovered for the story of the Flood. It is true that the scholars who deciphered the cuneiform texts were quite familiar with allusions to it. As long ago as 1906, the late Dr. Hilprecht of Philadelphia, after his Nippur (Calnah) excavations, declared he had no doubt of the reality of the Deluge. But knowledge from such sources was very generally confused in the minds of the public with the cuneiform legends of the Flood. As early as 1872 George Smith read his translation of the Chaldean account to a London audience. It aroused great interest at the time; but its full significance, as well as those of later discoveries of cuneiform versions, have been explained away by the conjectures of the higher critical school of thought, obsessed with theories that identified traditions with myths.

It was in the winter of 1928-9 that Dr. Langdon's expedition working at Kish, near Babylon, and Dr. Woolley's expedition excavating further south at Ur of the Chaldees, simultaneously came across the deposits left by a great Deluge.

The excavations at Kish have revealed two distinct

flood strata, one nineteen feet below the other. Dr. Langdon associates the Ur deposits with the lower level one at Kish. So let us turn to Dr. Woolley's account of his discovery. We are indebted to his book, *Ur of the Chaldees*, for the following extract:

"The shafts went deeper and suddenly the character of the soil changed. Instead of the stratified pottery and rubbish we were in perfectly clean clay, uniform throughout, the texture of which showed that it had been laid there by water. The workmen declared we had come to the bottom of everything, to the river silt. . . . I sent the men back to deepen the hole. The clean clay continued without change until it had attained a thickness of a little over eight feet. Then, as suddenly as it had begun, it stopped, and we were once more in layers of rubbish full of stone implements and pottery. . . . The great bed of clay marked, if it did not cause a break in, the continuity of history; above it we had the pure Sumerian civilization slowly developing on its own lines; below it there was a mixed culture . . . no ordinary rising of the rivers would leave behind it anything approaching the bulk of this clay bank; eight feet of sediment imply a very great depth of water, and the flood which deposited it must have been of a magnitude unparalleled in local history. That it was so is further proved by the fact that the clay bank marks a definite break in the continuity of the local culture; a whole civilization which existed before it is lacking above it and seems to have been submerged by the waters . . . there could be no doubt that the flood was the Flood of Sumerian history and legend, the flood on which is based the story of Noah."

This impressive account testifies to the reality of the

Flood, but leaves us uncertain of its extent. The very natural reaction which must be felt against those critical theories which have minimized the magnitude of the catastrophe, need not lead us to believe that it was universal, or that one solitary vessel once contained all that was left of humanity, birds, beasts and reptiles. At the same time a really balanced judgment must confess that the legends of a great Deluge that come from all parts of the world have their significance. It has been suggested that while they may not apply to a universal Flood, they certainly presume a general Dispersion by the descendants of those who experienced the Bible one.

It is interesting to reflect upon the dimensions of the Ark. Calculations have been made by sailors that it must have been larger than the figures given in the Genesis narrative. There its length would not be greater than an average Atlantic liner. But there seems some element of uncertainty regarding the length of the cubit referred to in the narrative. And the Babylonian account gives dimensions about twice the size of those recorded in Genesis. In that case the Ark might have been a good deal larger than the new *Queen Mary*.

The correct date of the Deluge is also uncertain. In the days of Abraham the current knowledge of when the catastrophe occurred appears to be reflected down to us on the clay prism illustrated here. After stating that those before the Flood ruled 241,200 years, the prism continues:

"The Deluge came up (upon the Land).
  After the Deluge had come,
  The Rulership which descended from heaven.
  [*Sic!*]
  At Kish there was the rulership
  At Kish . . . Gaur
  Became king"
                    (*vide Weld Blundell Collection*, vol. ii.).

The first dynasty of Kish is fixed at about 5500 B.C., and that of Ur at about 4100 B.C. As neither of these cities' names are included among those said to be in existence before the Flood, it would seem to have happened long before Abraham.

On the other hand, the Hebrew text of Genesis implies that Abraham was born only two hundred and ninety-two years after the Flood. Estimates made on this basis would place the Flood at about 2400 B.C. The Septuagint version of Genesis (translated into Greek from the Hebrew about 300 B.C.), represents Abraham as being born 1072 years after the Flood, which would bring the date up to about 3200 B.C. So far as the evidence of cuneiform literature carries us up to the present, it would seem as though chronology, recorded in the Old Testament, was uncertain before the days of Abraham. But our readers will shortly have occasion to remark that after the patriarch's time there appears to emerge a far more definite series of dates.

The use of the name Semitic (*i.e.* descendant of Shem, one of the sons of Noah) presupposes a connection with events *after* the Flood, since on this basis there could have been no Semites before the Deluge.

CHRONOLOGICAL CUNEIFORM CLAY PRISM

Written near Ur of the Chaldees when Abraham was actually alive. Its contents are frequently referred to in these pages.

(*By courtesy of the Ashmolean Museum, Oxford.*)

The actual cuneiform accounts of the Deluge have often been quoted and compared with the Bible narrative. The oldest found up to the present is on a tablet from Nippur written before 2200 B.C. So this knowledge must also antedate Abraham. It is evident that these versions are related to the Genesis account. But the presumption that the Bible version is of necessity derived from them, seems too hasty a decision in the light of the discoveries of the last ten years. Indeed since Monotheism proves to have been the original religion, the Genesis accounts of the Flood should be the original ones. The polytheistic character of the cuneiform versions stamp them as corrupted versions. It is of course true that a monotheistic account of Noah's flood, written in cuneiform, has not yet been found; or if found, not yet deciphered and published. But the wealth of material is so great, decipherment is so slow, and so much more must still be buried in the many unexplored areas, that no adverse conclusion is possible. It is probable that our generation has only reached the fringe of the knowledge which those who lived before and after Abraham have left behind them.

The late Professor Fessenden of the University of Pittsburg, in the year 1923, published a book entitled *The Deluged Civilization of the Caucasus Isthmus.*

This was favourably reviewed in 1924 by Sir Flinders Petrie in an article in *Ancient Egypt* entitled "The Caucasian Atlantis and Egypt." Professor Fessenden advanced a great deal of valuable evidence from the various deluge traditions, and from classical sources, in proof that they all refer to the Black Sea or adjacent country. He cites geologists for evidence that an ocean once existed from the Caucasus to Mongolia about 1850 miles in extent. For further information about this Eurasian, Mediterranean, or Sarmatian Ocean, readers are referred to the article "Caspian Sea" in the *Encyclopædia Britannica*. Professor Fessenden contended that even as late as 200 B.C. the Caspian and Aral Seas were connected. This ocean, which he calls the Ocean of Atlantis, was separated from the Black Sea on its eastern side by an isthmus of land.

Through causes which are suggested, but remain uncertain, the contents of this ocean were poured into the Black Sea, and Noah's deluge was the result.

Since the Deluge now begins to emerge as a real event in history, so the outlines of the Dispersion of Noah's descendants also begin to be discernible. But as yet there seem no clear conclusions from archæological evidence concerning events that happened immediately after the Flood. We must remember that it is only within the last six years that the Flood has been brought into the region of reality. And the mistake about the original religion has created confusion.

The three sons of Noah—Shem, Ham and Japheth—and the genealogies of their descendants, are set down in the tenth chapter of the Book of Genesis.

Many commentators have in the past agreed that the various names are geographical connections rather than ethnological relations; in other words, that this chapter outlines maps and not pedigrees. This assumption seems to ignore the natural initial tendency of first the members of the same family, and then those of the same race, to keep together. Assuming that the dispersal was as real an event as the Flood, is there anything unnatural about the statements in Genesis x.? Historically the period is very obscure, and it is only safe to generalize. When the panorama of races is viewed as a whole backwards towards these remote times, there seem to emerge three main groups of races that have inhabited the world since post-diluvian times. It is also not without significance that the neighbourhood of the Caucasus Mountains should be indicated by historians in our own times, as well as by relics of remote times, for the original homeland of our own, and many other races. That is just about where the Bible tells us Noah's Ark came to rest.

According to the Bible, the migration of the three sons of Noah would appear to have originally been: south in the case of Shem, south and south-west in that of Ham, and west in that of Japheth. In other words, Shem's descendants went to Arabia and the Persian Gulf, Ham's occupied Asia Minor and Africa, and Japheth's migrated towards Europe and the southern shores of the Black Sea. But it will be noticed in the narrative of Genesis x. that the so-called descendants of Ham were the first to develop under the leadership of Nimrod, and to found cities in the land of Shinar, and of Assyria. It may be that these were the Sumerians who inherited the great civilization which existed before the Flood. Ham's son Mizraim

73

has been identified with Egypt, while a portion of his race is also located in Southern Arabia in places which are named in the genealogy of Shem.

Higher Critics have represented the grouping of the nations in this chapter as due to prejudice. That is a reckless charge to make in the present state of our knowledge. A scrutiny of the text suggests, however, that it has been damaged in transmission. The tenth verse represents Nimrod as founding four great cities in the land of Shinar, and the eleventh verse, four more cities in the land of Assyria; but the Septuagint version transcribes the later passage "Out of that land went forth Asshur," and founded the latter cities. The Septuagint version appears to be correct; and the abrupt introduction of Asshur into the narrative suggests that some of the original has at any rate been misplaced; for Asshur is represented in the twenty-second verse as one of the sons of Shem.

But even accepting the text as it stands, a survey of very recent conclusions of scholars regarding the distribution of races, serves to enhance the significance of it, although writers seem too influenced by their unbeliefs to accept their results as a whole. But it has to be remarked again that the Caucasus is still identified as the homeland of civilization. No more satisfactory name seems to be found for the western races than Japhetic, while the Semites and Hamites are not in doubt. The discrepancies turn upon the identification of Elam with the Semites, and the uncertainty regarding who were the Sumerians. The Canaanite relationship to Ham is cleared up in the chapter on the Shepherd Kings; and both this race's culture as well as that of Egypt, probably came from foreigners. The grouping of the descendants of Japheth is further outlined in the chapter on Phœnician origins; it seems to satisfy evidence.

Reference has already been made to Professor Fessenden's theory of the Deluge. His evidence for the Dispersion is still more valuable. Herodotus is his authority for insisting on the close resemblance between the Colchians, who lived south of the Caucasus, and the Egyptians, both in looks, customs, and products.

Petrie fully confirms the fact that the Badarian or prehistoric civilization of Egypt, which he discovered, resembles the Solutrean culture of Europe, and contends that it must have travelled down from the Caucasus.

Petrie further confirms statements made by Professor Fessenden concerning the Egyptian Book of the Dead. He writes:

"In the Book of the Dead, the sun is said to rise over the mountains of Bakhau, and the modern Baku is at the eastern extremity of the Caucasus. The sun is said to set in Tamanu, and the Taman peninsula is at the western end of the Caucasus. . . . In the Caucasus region the natural fires of petroleum springs, both in the west at Batoum, in Colchis, and in the east at Baku on the Caspian, are claimed as the original idea of the lakes of fire in the Book of the Dead."

It is interesting also to notice that Professor Fessenden draws extensively on Greek mythology to prove that this civilization also came from the Caucasus. The

75

Odyssey, for example, is said to be a veritable guide book to the petroleum regions.

Sir Flinders takes up the subject again in *Ancient Egypt* (June 1926) in an article entitled "Origin of the Book of the Dead," and after citing many more examples of similarity of names remarks:

"This list accounts for most of the important names of places in the mythology of the Book of the Dead."

Knowledge still seems lacking of the very early civilization of Arabia, and what information is possessed of its remote past warns us that the country must be taken into account. It is a matter of common knowledge among scholars that a great civilization once existed in South Arabia, and the interior of this country is one of the least-known regions of the world. In 1930, Mr. Bertram Thomas, in his journey across the Southern Desert, heard rumours of the ruined city of Ubar, and saw extensive old caravan tracks leading to its supposed site.

In March 1934, a report appeared in the Press that M. Malraux, a French aviator, had discovered a city, still intact, which he identified with Saba (Sheba). It is said to be about eighty miles north of Mareb, which in turn is north of Aden at the south end of the Red Sea. M. Malraux is reported to have gained glimpses of twenty or more square towers or temples of a Semitic type of architecture. Photographs of these ruins taken from the air through the courtesy of the London correspondent of *L'Intransigeant*, have been seen by

AERIAL PHOTOGRAPH OF MYSTERIOUS RUINS IN THE INTERIOR OF ARABIA

Thought to be those of the ancient city of Saba, and said to be of white marble. Photographed by M. Malraux.

(Courtesy of "Intransigeant" of Paris.)

the author. One is reproduced here, and it is to be hoped that someone may soon be able to examine these remains, and photograph them from the ground.

These two reports seem to summarize recent news of the interior of Arabia. From more accessible parts, and from near the coast, there have come earlier evidences of Minean, Sabean, and Qatabanian inscriptions. The oldest form of the Semitic language at present known is the Accadian, and linguistically these three are closely allied to it. But it has been thought that the Minæan monuments in the Yemen do not date before about 1000 B.C. Behind these there is nevertheless evidence of a far older civilization. And authorities on the subject have long believed that here in Arabia might be found the original home of the Semitic race.

It has already been suggested that the world-wide traditions of the Flood may be accounted for by a world-wide Dispersion. And if it be assumed that the effect of the Flood was to restore some sort of Monotheism, it is interesting to consider whether the evidences of that religion, in both the Sumerian and Semitic races, as well as in the Egyptian religion, and in the European races, afford evidence that they all originally sprung from the same parentage. This association of religious ideas seems to suit the conditions postulated after the Flood, and expressed in the text:

"The whole earth was of one language and one speech." (Gen. xi. 1.)

And it accords with the confusion of deities, as well as tongues, that followed.

Interesting efforts have been made to prove that all languages can ultimately be traced to one source. That is a subject which cannot be examined within the limits of this volume, but is not without significance.

VII

THE COMING OF THE SHEPHERD KINGS

THOSE of our readers acquainted with the outlines of Egyptian history, will recall that before the advent of the eighteenth dynasty, Egypt was ruled, for an uncertain period of time, by mysterious peoples called the Hyksos, which the Egyptian historian Manetho said meant "Shepherd Kings." A great deal has been learned about these people through the excavations of the last six years. And whereas the Hyksos used to belong to Egyptian history alone, it has now become evident that they also ruled Syria and Palestine for an even longer time than they ruled Egypt.

According to the Egyptian historian Manetho, the Hyksos possessed Egypt for five hundred and eleven years. Modern German critics have seriously questioned such a long period of time, and reduced it to about one hundred years. Needless to say, other writers have followed their example! It is difficult to see how correct history can be written at all, when there is such presumptuous disregard of old historians. After all Manetho lived some two thousand years nearer the Hyksos times than our modern critics. Moreover, it seems quite improbable that an Egyptian historian would magnify what was to him a shameful period of Egyptian history.

During the last eight years Sir Flinders Petrie has excavated Hyksos sites on the borders of Egypt and Palestine, at Gerar, Bethphelet, and now at Old Gaza. Readers are asked to glance at the map. It was also Sir Flinders who, years ago, discovered and excavated the great camp of Avaris in Egypt, the last stronghold of these Shepherd Kings before they were finally expelled by a native Egyptian dynasty. Of all Egyptologists he must be regarded as being most familiar with the evidence left by the Hyksos, and he has established a personal contact with the remains of this civilization possessed by no other authority. Backed as his evidence is by the authority of Manetho, it seems idle for others any longer to contend that the Hyksos can be dismissed with a mere century of rule.

The real historical facts appear to be that at the end of the twelfth dynasty of Egypt, the Hyksos invaded the country, and drove the native dynasties up the Nile. And that the thirteenth, fourteenth, and seventeenth dynasties became contemporary with the fifteenth and sixteenth. Sir Flinders has worked out the following reckoning:

EGYPTIANS

XIII. 60 kings, 451 years . 2371–1918 B.C.
XIV. 76 kings, 184 years . 1918–1734 B.C.
XVII. 43 kings, 151 years . 1734–1583 B.C.

COMING OF THE SHEPHERD KINGS

HYKSOS

XV.	6 kings, 260 years	.	2371–2111 B.C.
XVI.	32 kings, 518 years	.	2111–1593 B.C.
	Kames 10 (?) years	.	1593–1583 B.C.

(*Vide* "A Revision of History," from *Ancient Egypt*,
March 1931.)

In the course of his excavations, Sir Flinders has
found thirty-eight scarabs or seals engraved with the
names of the Egyptian kings of the fifteenth and
sixteenth dynasties, and he is satisfied that these were
all Hyksos. Illustrations of thirty-six scarabs are given
in the above article.

So Hyksos rule of Egypt began in 2371 B.C. and
lasted to 1583 B.C. This more than substantiates
Manetho, who, as an Egyptian, would naturally
minimize the length of rule of invaders execrated in his
writing; and such establishment of the Hyksos domination over Egypt for such a long period, must seriously
react upon the ancient history of Palestine, as presented
to the public by recent writers.

The landmarks of their occupation which the Shepherd Kings have left behind them, consist of a peculiar
type of fortification. They seem to have recognized
that the summit of a perpendicular wall was not an
ideal vantage ground from which to shoot arrows, or
sling stones, to check the close approach of an enemy.
So the Hyksos protected their settlements by a sloping
rampart or glacis with a ditch, which exposed assailants
to a direct hail of arrows and stones at every point

of their advance. This type of fortification first became noticeable on the site of their stronghold Avaris (*Tel-el-Yahudiyeh*), inside which the Egyptian historian Manetho says they made their last stand before their final expulsion from Egypt by the eighteenth dynasty. Similar systems of fortification have since been discovered, at Quatna in Syria, at Hazor in North Palestine by Garstang, at Shechem in Central Palestine by Welter, at Debir or Kerjath Sephir by Albright, at Tell Duweir (or Lachish) by Starkey, and in the older fortification of Jericho by Garstang. There must, of course, be added to this list the frontier fortress of Bethphelet, and ancient Gaza. Excavations of other sites in Syria and Palestine will doubtless add to this list. But sufficient have now been found to justify the conclusion that the Shepherd Kings conquered, and occupied, Syria and Palestine, as well as Egypt. That their period of occupation was as long, and even longer, than their occupation of Egypt, is evidenced by the fact that it was through Syria and Palestine their invasion of Egypt was made; and according to Manetho, it was into Palestine that the remnants of these Shepherd Kings were driven on their final expulsion from Egypt.

In the light of his recent excavations at Old Gaza, Sir Flinders Petrie has also come to the conclusion that the Hyksos were the first to introduce the horse to Egypt. It is probable that they originated the horses and chariots, which figure so often in the Old Testament, and that these weapons of warfare facilitated their conquest of Syria, Palestine, and Egypt. The problem of the identity of these Hyksos or Shepherd Kings has long been puzzling historians.

The word "Hyksos" means Royal Shasu, and the word "Shasu," in Egyptian, always refers to the Bedouin or Arabs. Josephus, the Jewish historian, was an eyewitness of the siege of Jerusalem by Titus in A.D. 70. He wrote much about the Old Testament. Among other writings which have survived are his Essays *contra Apion*. In these he calls the Shepherd Kings "our ancestors"—that is, of course, the ancestors of the tribe of Judah, one of the twelve tribes of Israel. All these twelve tribes were in turn descended from Abraham, who is designated in the Bible as "Abram, the Hebrew" (Gen. xiv. 13). But as the Hyksos occupation of Egypt extended from 2371–1583 B.C., and as it has already been stated and will later be proved, that Abraham was born about 2160 B.C., it is evident that when Josephus calls the Shepherd Kings "our ancestors," he refers not to the Israelites, but to their ancestors the Hebrews. We are all so accustomed to associate the Israelites with the Hebrews, that we overlook the fact that there were other Hebrews besides Abraham; and judging from Genesis xxv. 2, other Hebrews that sprung from Abraham besides the Israelites.

The name "Hebrew" occurs again at a later period in the Book of Genesis. In those delightful stories about Joseph in Egypt, he too is designated as a Hebrew; and when he was brought before Pharaoh to interpret that king's dream, he is represented as saying:

"Indeed, I was stolen away out of the land of the Hebrews." (Gen. xl. 15.)

How came Canaan to be called the land of the Hebrews? The description could scarcely be derived from the residence there of Jacob and his twelve sons. It suggests that there were other Hebrews in Canaan, and probably a considerable number of them, besides Jacob and his children. It even suggests that the ruling race had not been Canaanites at all, but Hebrews.

There is another statement of the Jewish historian, Josephus, regarding these Shepherd Kings. He writes, "Some say they were Arabs." That, of course, goes to confirm the interpretation of the word "Hyksos," to which allusion has already been made. Here it should be pointed out that both Hebrews and Arabs were Semites; in other words, they were branches of the various races descended from Noah's son Shem. And attention is going to be drawn to evidence of the presence of Arabs speaking archaic Hebrew in South Palestine apparently before the days of Joseph.

The excavations at Old Gaza, to which fuller reference will be made in a succeeding chapter, reveal an advanced civilization in that city, or rather in the series of five cities which Sir Flinders Petrie has found superimposed one above the other. The first or lowest of these may date back as far as 3000 B.C., the third belongs to the period 2371–2111 B.C., the last only to the time when the Hyksos were expelled from Egypt.

In Chapter III, which deals with the geography of Palestine, reference has already been made to the fact that in the Great War, Lord Allenby invaded the country from Egypt, using Gaza on the west and Jericho on the east, as his bases of operation. Conversely, it may be suggested that if Old Gaza was the base of operations from which the Hyksos invaded Egypt on the west, excavators might be able to find traces of them at Jericho on the east.

And this has proved to be the case. Professor Garstang's report of his last excavation of Jericho in 1933, reveals the fact that beneath the city destroyed by Joshua, he has found the remains of three other cities superimposed on each other, with quantities of Hyksos scarabs in the Palace area, and in the tombs. He describes the wall of the oldest of these cities as being "built of large slabs of clay banded with thick layers of bituminous earth after a Babylonian fashion." In the next city also he found evidence of Babylonian influence, while to the third belonged the type of fortification identified with the Hyksos period. Before endeavouring to draw conclusions, two other pieces of evidence require some attention.

The first is from Old Gaza whose culture Sir Flinders Petrie describes as Elamite. To-day Elam is known as Persia. Excavations are just beginning to be made there. A few months ago illustrations of the marvellous bas-reliefs found on the walls of the palace of King Darius, at Persepolis, were published in this country, and the announcement of the find of 20,000 cuneiform tablets. King Darius, of course, lived some centuries before Christ and a great many centuries after Abraham.

But the trend of discovery points towards modern Persia, formerly ancient Elam, for the early art centre of the world; and that even the superb art of the Greeks all came from that quarter. What possibilities, therefore, do excavations such as the above present for an increase in the world's knowledge! The confidence of those who thought we already knew all about ancient history has been misplaced.

In the previous chapter reference was made to the distribution of the descendants of Noah's three sons—Shem, Ham and Japheth—as recorded in Genesis x. A further reference to this chapter will reveal the fact that Elam was there represented to be the eldest son of Shem (Gen. x. 22). And a glance at the map on p. 56 shows that the country of Elam adjoins Babylonia, consequently there would be a close affinity between the culture of the two countries.

The other piece of evidence to which some allusion has already been made in this chapter, comes from the newly deciphered Ras Shamra tablets. Although these inscriptions were found some hundreds of miles north of Jericho, yet the writers of them represent themselves as Arabs coming from the Arabah or country south of Jericho. No attempt to fix the date of this migration appears to have yet been made by the French experts. But the mythology inscribed on the tablets refers to the birth of Shalem, the son of Terach, the Moon-God, in the Wilderness of Kadesh, a locality familiar to us in connection with the wanderings of the Children of Israel under Moses.

Now this god Shalem seems to have given his name to Jerusalem, or Uru-Salem; and as far back as the time of Abraham there is a reference to Melchizedek king *of Safem*. It is reasonable, therefore, to infer that the tradition of these Arabs speaking archaic Hebrew, but living in Syria in the days of Joshua, goes back to a time before Abraham when their ancestors were residing in the extreme south of Palestine. And the further inference may be made that, since Babylonians and Arabs and Hebrews were all descendants of Shem, there is considerable evidence of Semitic occupation of Syria and Palestine, even before the days of Abraham.

The relation of Babylonia, with its Elamite culture, to the Semitic race requires further elucidation. Mention has already been made that its earliest inhabitants were Sumerians and Semites. The latter race began to come into prominence about 2800 B.C., and in the course of the next fifty years it produced the great conqueror Sargon of Agade. In his youth, Sargon was a priest in a Sumerian temple; he rose to be, perhaps, the first great military conqueror of the then known world. His date has been quite definitely fixed by Dr. Langdon at 2752 B.C. He left behind him inscriptions from which it is thought that he penetrated even to the Mediterranean and conquered North Syria. His successor, Naram Sin, certainly did so. Here, then, began the supremacy of the Semitic race which resulted in a long line of kings of Semitic origin sitting upon the throne of Babylonia and adjacent countries.

This great irruption of Semitic conquest absorbed the Sumerian Babylonian civilization. The evidence that it penetrated through Palestine has already been noticed. The excavations at Old Gaza still in progress, and those at Jericho, supply this important information. Here on the borders of Egypt are relics of a very ancient civilization that is not Egyptian. Garstang at Jericho says the walls of even its first city, to which he assigns a date of from 2500 B.C., were built in Babylonian style. While Petrie at Old Gaza dates his first two cities even earlier, and describes the culture as Elamite. Through its geographical position at the south end of the coastland corridor leading to Egypt, and through its being also a seaport, Old Gaza was a far more important place than Jericho, for it was about twenty times the size.

All the evidence is not clear as to when the actual Hyksos occupation of Palestine began. Petrie at any rate would assign a date of about 2371 B.C. for these Shepherd Kings' conquest of Egypt, and there seems a possibility that there were two distinct Hyksos periods—Early and Late. While again the Semitic Babylonian occupation of Palestine appears to have preceded the coming of the Shepherd Kings. There were thus two or even three great streams of Semitic occupation, the former from the east and north, and the latter from Arabia in the south.

So the evidence as a whole suggests that those who brought the cuneiform system of writing and the Hebrew language into Palestine were Semites. In the course of their long occupation these Semites inter-married with the Canaanites and Amorites and the other inferior races who were the earlier occupants of the land.

The Tel el Amarna cuneiform letters already men-tioned testify to the permanence of this civilization. They were written by the petty kings of Palestine and Syria to the two Pharaohs who reigned in the period 1400–1360 B.C. It is significant that although Palestine and Syria had been completely conquered and ruled by the Egyptians for some eighty years before these letters were written, yet neither the Egyptian script, nor the Egyptian language, were used in addressing their Egyptian Suzerain.

The evidence of the Ras Shamra tablets suggests the use of archaic Hebrew by Arabs in South Palestine before 2100 B.C.; and the descendants of these Arabs were still speaking that language far up the coast of Syria at the same time when the Tel el Amarna tablets were despatched to Egypt. To sum up the contents of this chapter, it has been recognized for some time that when Abraham left Ur of the Chaldees he left a country which had long been ruled by his race. But it is only now beginning to be realized that, when he came into Canaan, he was in a country which had been invaded, and occupied, and traversed, by others of his race, on their way to the conquest of Egypt. It has been customary to compare the Hyksos with the Bedouin Arab: the traces he has left now suggest that he more nearly resembled the Saracen. His was a Semitic aristocracy correctly described by Hyksos, or Royal Bedouin.

On the other hand, the land of Canaan takes its name from Canaan, the son of Ham, on whom a curse was placed by Noah:

"Cursed be Canaan; a servant of servants shall he be unto his brethren. . . . Blessed be the Lord God of Shem, and let Canaan be his servant. God shall enlarge Japheth, and let him dwell in the tents of Shem; and Canaan shall be his servant." (Gen. ix. 25–27.)

In the next chapter it is written:

"And Canaan begat Zidon his first born, and Heth, and the Jebusite and the Amorite . . . and the border of the Canaanites was from Zidon, as thou comest to Gerar, unto Gaza; as thou goest, unto Sodom, and Gomorrah, and Admah, and Zeboim even unto Lasha." (Gen. x. 15–19.)

The Babylonian cuneiform tablets record the fact that the very word Amurru, or Amorite, actually became a class name for labourers. A tablet found at Lagash actually specifies other and different nationalities in a list of workmen styled "Amurru" (*vide Cambridge Ancient History*, vol. i., 420).

Bible students have often wondered how it came about that these fellahin races acquired the civilization and the power which they possessed by the time of Joshua. The very early conquest of the country by the Semitic races explain these phenomena. As already pointed out, the conquerors found Canaan occupied by primitive native races, and they imposed upon them their language, and the arts and civilization originally acquired in Mesopotamia. Those Semites who settled in the country, or who were ultimately driven out of Egypt, became absorbed in these native races.

But it will be noticed that the verses quoted above include the descendants of Japheth as dwelling in the tents of Shem, and also using the labour of Canaan. So account must be taken of their presence.

VIII

PHŒNICIAN ORIGINS

THE Phœnician people occupied the coastland, in the north of Canaan and along the whole of Syria, for about two hundred miles; Tyre, Sidon, and Arvad were their principal seaports. They were the navigators of the world in Bible times, and founded colonies. Carthage, on the coast of Africa, opposite Italy, was their great settlement; but they extended their colonization as far west as Tartessos in Spain; and they have left ample traces of their presence at Cadiz; whence they sailed their ships to Cornwall, and probably to other parts of Britain, and even, as will be suggested, to Ireland.

It is less than ten years since the development of Phœnicia was placed at about 600 B.C., and Phœnician claims to a far earlier civilization were attributed to a desire to emulate the Egyptians. To-day it is clear that such claims were correct.

Phœnician culture was of an advanced type, and the alphabet has been regarded as their invaluable contribution to civilization. Until quite recently the earliest date ascribed to alphabetical writing was somewhere about 900 B.C. The earliest example on the tomb of Ahiram king of Gebal was attributed to a much later date than Rameses II (1295–1229 B.C.). The discovery just made of the writing on the ewer found at Tell Duweir in Palestine, among strata that cannot be later than Rameses II, now establishes that date; while the alphabetic cuneiform inscriptions found at Ras Shamra in Northern Phœnicia, carries alphabetical writing there back another century. But as will be seen later, the earliest alphabetical writing found, came from the Peninsula of Sinai and may date back several hundred years more.

The principal account of Phœnician origin was derived from Herodotus (430 B.C.), the celebrated Greek historian, on whom the world has had so much to rely for a knowledge of ancient history. Herodotus wrote:

"This people, who had formerly dwelt on the shores of the Erythrean Sea, having migrated to the Mediterranean and settled in the parts which they now inhabit, began at once, they say, to adventure on long voyages, freighting their vessels with the wares of Egypt and Assyria."

The Erythrean Sea is generally taken to mean the Red Sea, but some would transfer the title to the Persian Gulf. On the whole the evidence seems to suggest that the Red Sea and its eastern arm the Gulf of Akaba is the correct interpretation. Herodotus dated the founding of Tyre at 2756 B.C., but until recent discoveries such antiquity was not credited.

Now, however, the tablets found at Ras Shamra on the coast of what was ancient Phœnicia, both directly and indirectly presume an early date.

In the previous chapter about the Shepherd Kings, reference is made to the great Babylonian Semitic conqueror Sargon, whose date 2752 B.C. has been fairly well established.

If Sargon penetrated to the Mediterranean and conquered North Syria, then the statement of Herodotus that Tyre was founded in 2756 B.C. will be correct.

In the passage previously quoted, Herodotus represents the Phœnicians as coming from the shores of the Erythrean Sea; and whether this means the Red Sea, or the Persian Gulf, the reference contains a suggestion of their original Semitic origin. The Phœnicians do not appear under that name in the Bible, with the exception of Christ's healing of the Syrophœnician woman. But they nevertheless come into the Old Testament under such designations as—"the inhabitants of Tyre," or "of Zidon" or "Arvad."

Bible students will also remember the close relations that King Solomon had with Hiram king of Tyre, in the building of the Temple at Jerusalem. At the conclusion of the last chapter, quotations were made from Genesis ix. concerning the Canaanites, and it may be noticed that their northern border extended to the Phœnician city of Zidon. But it is suggested that, as in Palestine, these Canaanites were fellahin, and were only responsible for any civilization that existed before the occupation of their country by Semites.

Syria was the country behind the Phœnician coastlands. A later chapter will discuss the subject of

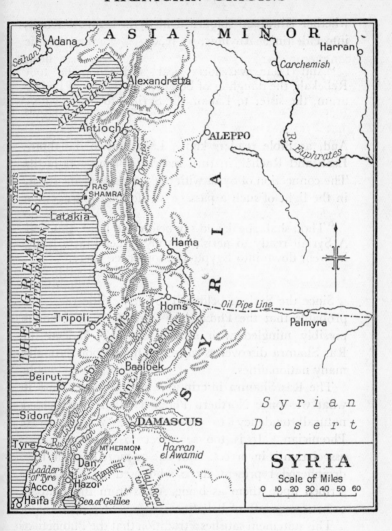

95

whether Abraham sojourned in Syria before he came into Palestine. Anyhow, we read:

"And Isaac was forty years old when he took Rebekah, the daughter of Bethuel, the Syrian of Padan-aram, the sister to Laban, the Syrian, to be his wife."
(Gen. xxv. 20.)

And, as Bible readers know, Laban's two daughters, Leah and Rachel, in turn married Isaac's son Jacob. The connection of Syria with the Israelites seems strong in the light of such a passage as the following:

"Thou shalt speak and say before the Lord, thy God, A Syrian ready to perish was my father [Jacob], and he went down into Egypt, and sojourned there."
(Deut. xxvi. 5.)

Since the Syrians belonged to the Semitic race, it is probable that the Phœnicians were the same, though possibly mingled with other elements. Indeed the Ras Shamra discoveries suggest a mixed population of many nationalities.

The Ras Shamra inscriptions having been found in what was once Northern Phœnicia, there has been a natural tendency to assume these writings were Phœnician. It is too soon yet to assert that this association is incorrect. But one or more of the tablets deciphered represent those who used the rituals inscribed upon them as being Arabs from the Arabah, or extreme south of Palestine.

This statement satisfies a tradition that the Phœnicians

were a people who fled from the neighbourhood of the Dead Sea, in consequence of the cataclysm that occurred in Abraham's time, associated with the destruction of Sodom and Gomorrah.

In a later chapter it will be seen that the Ras Shamra tablets contain much with which we are familiar through the earlier books in the Bible, but mixed up with it is the gross polytheism and mythology already associated in our minds with Phœnicia, and familiar to us through Greek sources.

These Ras Shamra inscriptions of 1400–1350 B.C. incidentally confirm the authenticity of the writings of the Phœnician sage, Sanchuniathon.

Critics have regarded Sanchuniathon's writings as a forgery on the part of the Greek writer Philo Byblus; the Ras Shamra discovery suggests them to be genuine.

The date of Sanchuniathon is variously placed from before the Siege of Troy (1197 B.C.) to about 900 B.C. He claimed to have had access to inscriptions of a much earlier date. Indeed his account leads one to believe that he had searched out history written by Thoth, the Egyptian god of writing. He mentions Adam and Eve under the names Aion and Hawwa, and alludes indirectly to the Temptation. Here it should be recorded that a Ras Shamra tablet also mentions Adam; it describes him as "the Man from the East," but it does not, as was originally reported, mention Eve.

Sanchuniathon's statements, in the light of Ras

Shamra, become of new importance for the study of Greek mythology. They convey the impression that the gods and demi-gods, familiar to us in the Classics, mostly came from Asia Minor.

It would now seem as though this location for the home of classical mythology is a correct one; and further, that in some cases at least, the Greek and Roman deities and demi-gods once lived on the earth as human beings, and were afterwards deified. The curious passage about the offspring of the intercourse between the sons of God and daughters of men (Gen. vi. 4) tends to support such a conjecture.

But to revert to Sanchuniathon. He describes the Creation, and the ten generations of men following it, in terms which bear resemblances to both the Biblical and Babylonian accounts. Though nothing seems to be said about the Flood in these polytheistic records, there appears to be a break at the tenth generation, which suggests correspondence with the ten generations before the Flood recorded in the earlier chapters of Genesis; as well as with the eight generations recorded on the Babylonian cuneiform clay prism illustrated in this book.

In Sanchuniathon's writings there follows the statement:

"Generation 11. From these men were begot Misor and Sydyc, *i.e.* well freed and just. These found out the use of salt."

Dr. Langdon has pointed out that the word "Misor" should be Mishor—"Righteousness," and that the mistake is evidence that the writer was dealing with Babylonian names. In Babylonian mythology these two are attendants of the god—Shamash. It has been suggested that the passage, "Righteousness and justice are the habitation of thy throne," found in Psalm lxxxix. 14, may be related to this imagery.

Dr. Langdon remarks that among the Syrians, Phœnicians and Canaanites, "El" seems to have become a special name for Shamash.

But to continue:

"Generation 12. From Misor came Tautus who found out the writing of the first letters, whom the Egyptians call Thoor, the Alexandrians Thoyth, and the Greeks Hermes. But from Sydyc came the Dioscuri, or Cabiri, or Corybantes, or Samothraces. These he saith first invented the building a complete ship."

Thus the Cabiri appear to have been Semites. There are allusions to them in the Ras Shamra tablets, and they seem to have been demi-gods with an eighth brother Æsculapius.

Meanwhile it is interesting to notice that Breasted, the Egyptian historian, identifies Æsculapius with a certain Imhotep who lived in Egypt in the thirtieth century B.C., a time which, according to present calculations, is comparatively near to the Flood. In the Ras Shamra inscriptions this man's name appears as Eshmun.

The evidence of early intercourse with Egypt in ancient Phœnician writings is fully borne out by other archæological discoveries; and it is only what one would expect to be the case. The Phœnician seaports were but three or four days' sail from Old Gaza, on the Egyptian frontier, where Sir Flinders Petrie has found these five ancient cities superimposed one above each other. Sir Flinders claims that certain gold ornaments which he has dug up there in the strata, dated 1500 B.C., are of Irish manufacture. It has also been asserted that some blue paste beads, found at Stonehenge, and in various parts of Wiltshire, England, came from Egypt about the same early date. Were Phœnician ships the medium whereby this incredibly early trading was carried on with the far-distant shores of England and possibly Ireland? The connection of these two countries with Egypt, and with Asia Minor, at this remote period of time, when Moses was possibly living at the Egyptian court, receives some confirmation from tradition. But an age which despised traditions of a far more recent date could hardly be expected to take any notice of such stories.

A further problem that arises in connection with the early relations between the Phœnicians and Egypt is the part that they played in the invasion of the Shepherd Kings. As stated in the last chapter, there seems little doubt that the Hyksos were great horsemen, and we can hardly associate horsemanship with the dwellers on the coastland. But nevertheless it must be borne in mind that both the Phœnicians and the Shepherd Kings were branches of the same Semitic race, and the affinity between them probably made them allies. And again, there is the evidence of these Ras Shamra tablets that the ancestors of a people living in the north of Phœnicia were Arabs.

Writers have long laid emphasis on Egyptian rule and influence in Phœnicia, but the time has surely come when we must recognize the converse—Phœnician rule and influence in Egypt. Do the ruins of these great palaces Sir Flinders Petrie is excavating at Old Gaza, represent the ebb and flow of a Phœnician-Hyksos conquest of Egypt? Apparently this great Egyptian authority is reaching some such conclusions for he writes:

"The determinative of three water lines, MU, which accompanies seven names (*i.e.* on the Hyksos scarabs) would agree to their being seafarers, which is implied in the title of the sixteenth dynasty 'Hellenic shepherd kings,' as Hellene is the regular equivalent of maritime 'HA NEBU,' 'lords of the north.' The fifteenth dynasty is correctly named from Phœnicia, whence it entered Egypt" (*Ancient Egypt*—" A Revision of History ").

On the whole it would seem as though we must expect to find in Phœnicia a connection with the descendants of Japheth as well as with the Semites. We read:

"The sons of Japheth; Gomer, and Magog, and Madai, and Javan, and Tubal, and Meshech, and Tiras. And the sons of Gomer; Ashkenaz and Riphath and Togarmah. And the sons of Javan; Elishah, and Tarshish, Kittim and Dodanim. Of these were the isles of the nations divided in their lands, every one after his tongue; after their families, in their nations."

(Gen. x. 2–5.)

Josephus, the historian, writes that the descendants of Japheth inhabited Asia Minor and the south of Europe as far as Cadiz in Spain. From Gomer sprung the Gauls: from Magog the Scythians: from Madai the Medes: from Javan the Greeks: from Thiras the Thracians: from Meshech the Cappadocians: and from Tubal the Iberians. The sons of Javan certainly suggest Greeks, and Kittim is usually supposed to be Cyprus. The giant Japetos was their mythological ancestor, and his name has been identified with Japheth. The close connections between the seafaring Phœnicians and the Greeks has already been suggested. Before 1200 B.C. the tribe of Dan had become a seafaring people (Judges v. 17), and it has been claimed that they became associated with the Phœnicians, and even identified with them.

The Cabiri, according to Sanchuniathon, were connected with the island of Samothrace. Mr. Theodor Gaster of London, whose work on the Ras Shamra tablets in Paris enables him to speak with authority, says that these Cabiri are termed Agzarim on these ancient tablets, an Arabic word that means "islanders." They are also called "sons of the sea." Eshmun, whose name has been mentioned as the eighth of these heroes, was specially worshipped in Cyprus, and also in the island of Sardinia. This information about the Cabiri, and about Eshmun, is of importance to classical scholars, for they will notice that the Ras Shamra tablets settle a long disputed question; but as it is not of much interest to the general public, this brief notice must be sufficient. It is, however, useful, since it establishes the very close connection between the Phœnicians and the islands of the Mediterranean and their inhabitants, in remote times.

Thus recent evidence points to the conclusion that the Phœnicians were a mixed race.

IX

EVIDENCE ABOUT ABRAHAM

TWO great volumes of Ur excavations, entitled *The Royal Cemetery*, were published in 1934. With the aid of the British Museum several of its illustrations are reproduced in this chapter. How is it that people seem to miss the significance of such photographs, even amid the many distractions of modern life? First let us consider that the objects illustrated come from the place where Abraham lived in his youth; and then that they were made, and either worn or used, a thousand years before Abraham. And a thousand years is a very long time indeed! It is not even yet a thousand years since William the Conqueror landed in England, and fought the Battle of Hastings. We are accustomed to regard William and his Normans as civilized people, though somewhat barbarous. But do their tombs contain such evidences of art and culture as were buried in Ur of the Chaldees one thousand years before Abraham?

Lord Beaconsfield, when reproached in Parliament for his Jewish origin, is said to have replied: "My ancestors were princes before the noble lord's had emerged from breech clout." The school of critics and

THE GOLD HELMET OF MES-KALAM-DUG

A king who was buried at Ur of the Chaldees more than a thousand years before
Abraham lived there.

(Courtesy of Baghdad Museum.)

ILLUSTRATIONS OF GOLD BOWLS AND FLOWER VASES
Buried in the royal tombs of Ur of the Chaldees (3500–3150 B.C.).
(*Courtesy of British Museum.*)

evolutionists postulated something more primitive than breech clout for Abraham's ancestry. Such teaching becomes foolish in the face of such evidences of civilization from Ur of the Chaldees. It is by no means easy, rapidly to adjust one's outlook on the past, to an entirely different background from what we have been led to believe must have existed. Anything suggesting such a state of early civilization among classical writers has been treated as myth; but so far from early writers having over-estimated remote civilization they seem to have under-estimated it; and there is no ground left to discredit their statements about it. Let us try to regard Abraham as a man, reared and educated in an ancient city, amid a fine culture and civilization, who gave up town life and went to live in tents and to keep sheep, in Canaan.

The Bible represents Abraham to be descended from Shem, one of the three sons of Noah.

The genealogical record (which may be found in the eleventh chapter of Genesis) runs as follows: Shem, Arpachshad, Shelah, Eber, Peleg, Reu, Serug, Nahor, Terah, Abram (later re-named Abraham). The pedigree of Shem's descendants outlined in the previous chapter, opens with the words:

"Shem, the father of all the children of Eber."
(Gen. x. 21.)

This emphasizes the importance of Eber's descent, which four verses later is recorded as follows:

"And unto Eber were born two sons: the name of the one was Peleg (Division), for in his days was the earth divided, and his brother's name was Joktan."

(Gen. x. 25.)

The further study of the text discloses the fact that Abraham's descent came through Peleg, while Joktan was the father of a dozen sons whose names identify them as settling in South Arabia.

In the two previous chapters reference has been made to two main streams of Semitic migration into Syria and Palestine—the Semitic Babylonian and the Arabian. With the knowledge now at our disposal it seems evident that these two streams were the respective descendants of Peleg and Joktan, and grouped together, as a whole, under the general title "the children of Eber"—whence the word "Hebrew." If such be the case, then Abraham belonged to the Semitic-Babylonian branch, while the Shepherd Kings possibly came from the Arabian.

The following passage from the pen of Dr. Langdon casts a great deal of light on the early history of the Hebrews:

"The Hebrew deity El . . . whose name occurs quite regularly in the plural Elohim . . . is the god of the Habiru, a people who appear in various kingdoms and local city dynasties of Babylonia and Assyria from 2200 B.C. . . . I am entering on debatable ground here when I assume that the Hebrews and their god Illani (plural always written ideographically) are identical with the Habiru and their god Elohim. There seems no doubt at all that this was the case. . . .

Accepting this thesis, the Hebrews had served for six centuries as mercenary soldiers and traders among the Babylonians, Assyrians, etc. . . . before they entered and occupied Canaan" (*Semitic Mythology*).

It will be seen that this reference concerns the Hebrews of Joshua's time, as well as those of Abraham's, although six centuries divide them. Further reference will therefore be made to this quotation in connection with Joshua's conquest of Canaan. But at this earlier period our attention is directed to the original warlike character of the sons of Eber, in contrast to the peaceful occupation adopted by Abraham and his descendants. And it may also be noticed how this piece of evidence throws light on the other branch of the sons of Eber, the Arabians who became known as the Shepherd Kings.

So much, then, for Abraham's ancestry; of his more immediate relatives we read:

"Now these are the generations of Terah: Terah begat Abram, Nahor, and Haran; and Haran begat Lot. And Haran died before his father Terah in the land of his nativity, in Ur of the Chaldees. . . . And Terah took Abram, his son, and Lot, the son of Haran, his son's son, and Sarai, his daughter-in-law, his son Abram's wife; and they went forth with them from Ur of the Chaldees, to go into the land of Canaan; and they came unto Haran and dwelt there. And the days of Terah were two hundred and five years: and Terah died in Haran." (Gen. xi. 27–32.)

A critical study (for what it is worth) of this quotation, indicates a residence of Terah and his family at Ur of the Chaldees, from the birth till the death of his youngest son Haran. Since Haran lived to have a son Lot, the family must have been at Ur of the Chaldees for a considerable time. The passage is, in a way, remarkable, because it does not say that Abram himself was born there, although we infer that he was educated there. The apocryphal books of the Old Testament, such as the Book of Jasher, represent Terah to have been a great soldier and commander of the armies of the king of Babylon. And this would accord with the evidence of the inscriptions that the Habiru were mercenary soldiers.

It has been the fashion to treat with scorn any evidence from such sources; nevertheless a newly deciphered Ras Shamra tablet appears to record a remote conflict between Keret king of Sidon and the tribes of Zebulan and Asher, with Edomites, under the guidance of the moon-god Terach. If this be not an echo of some early Habiru conflict with Sidonians in which Terah was engaged, it nevertheless associates Abraham's descendants with Terah; and the fact that Ur of the Chaldees was a centre of the worship of the moon-god serves to complete the picture.

Thus this new evidence tends at any rate to support the reality of Abraham's relationship and his residence at Ur. It may be urged that the identification of Terah with moon-worship is both distasteful to our present-day beliefs, and damages the evidence that Monotheism was the original religion of the Semitic

HEAD-DRESS OF SHUB-AD

A queen who was buried at Ur of the Chaldees in the midst of the bodies of her maids of honour about the same time as Mes-Kalam-Dug, say, 3500–3150 B.C.

(Courtesy of British Museum.)

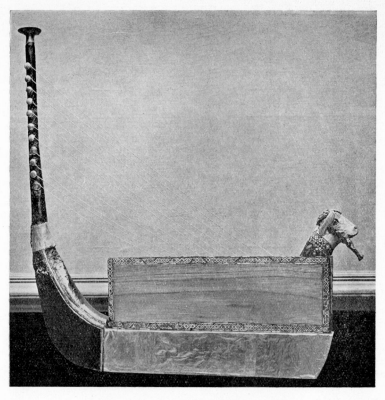

THE ELEVEN-STRINGED HARP OF QUEEN SHUB-AD

Found in the royal tombs of Ur. It must have been used nearly 2500 years before David referred to " the ten-stringed harp " in one of his Psalms.

(Courtesy of British Museum.)

race. Nevertheless it confirms what Joshua long after-wards told the Israelites:

"Your fathers dwelt of old beyond the River, even Terah, the father of Abraham, and the father of Nahor; *and they served other gods.*" (Joshua xxiv. 2.)

Reference has already been made to some of the discoveries at Ur of the Chaldees. It is a matter of common knowledge that Dr. Woolley has been ex-cavating there for eight years, and his discovery of the deposits left by the Flood have been already referred to in these pages. It would seem as though Abraham must have known all about these Flood deposits; he might even have seen them. Calculations indicate that the cuneiform clay prism with the chronology of kings before and after the Flood (see page 70) was actually written in his day. Those who have read Dr. Woolley's reports of his excavations will remember that he found, deep down in the soil, the royal interments of the ancient kings of Ur. And the illustrations of some of the objects buried with them, have been referred to at the beginning of this chapter. He also found, grouped around the royal remains, the fully clothed skeletons of soldiers, slaves, and maids of honour, who appear to have poisoned themselves, or been poisoned, in order that they might attend their royal master and mistress in the next world. Some evidence surely, however barbaric, of a belief in a future life!

Dr. Woolley's excavation of the interior of the city of Ur of the Chaldees, and his discoveries there, further change previous conceptions of the surroundings in

which Abram must have spent his earlier years. Dr.
Woolley tells us that in the great patriarch's day, the
citizens of Ur lived in houses built of walls of burnt
brick below, with mud brick above, the whole being
both plastered and white-washed. These houses were
two stories high, and contained as many as a dozen
and more rooms grouped round a central paved
courtyard.

The streets of the city were very narrow, and the
walls on either side lacked windows, for the houses
derived their light and air from the interior courtyards.
The inside of these dwelling-houses reminds us of our
own modern residences. There was the staircase to
the upper floor made of brick, it is true, rather than
wood; and there was the lavatory behind the staircase.
There was the kitchen with its fireplace, the reception-
room with its wider doors, the servants' hall and the
family chapel for worship. Against the rear wall of the
latter was a brick altar, with a shallow niche above, or
at the side, for clay images, or Teraphim, which may
perhaps be compared with the Lares and Penates of the
Romans. Under the floor of the chapel was a vaulted
tomb where members of the family were buried.

The education possessed by the inhabitants of these
houses was demonstrated by the occasional finds inside
them of cuneiform clay tablets: some were historical,
others were hymn-books, others dealt with mathematics,
or arithmetic. Among the latter there were even forms
for extracting both square and cube roots. It comes
as a shock to us that besides being able to read and

write, both Abram, and even Sarah, in the days of their youth might have suffered the same perplexities regarding cube roots as do our present-day students!

The suggestion that Abram discontinued his studies in cities and went into western lands, ruled at that time by men of his race, in order to keep sheep, may still serve as an example in our present time. The name Abraham, or rather Abram, is found in the Babylonian cuneiform contract tablets of about his era; it means "My father is high." A similar designation also occurs in South Arabia.

Our readers have already been promised further information as to the date that Abraham lived, and this seems a suitable place for it, although the chronology is derived from the Jericho excavations, which come later. After the publication of *The New Knowledge of the Old Testament*, it came as a surprise to find that the Jericho dating fitted the Bible narrative, before the Fall of Jericho, as well as it did after that event.

If the intervals of time are set down exactly as they are stated in the Old Testament, the following are the results:

Abraham was one hundred years old when
Isaac was born (Gen. xxi. 5) . . 100

Isaac was sixty years old when Jacob was
born (Gen. xxv. 26) 60

Jacob was one hundred and thirty years
old when he went down into Egypt
(Gen. xlvii. 9) 130

The Israelites were in Egypt four hundred and thirty years (Exod. xii. 40, 41) .	430
The Israelites wandered forty years in the Wilderness (Deut. ii. 7, etc.; Joshua v. 6)	40
Jericho was destroyed by Joshua (according to Professor Garstang's excavations) about	1400 B.C.
Birth of Abraham	2160 B.C.
From these figures, as Abraham came into Canaan when seventy-five years old (Gen. xii. 4), that event occurred . .	2085 B.C.
And as he was one hundred years old when Isaac was born, the latter was born	2060 B.C.
Sodom and Gomorrah were destroyed when Abraham was ninety-nine (Gen. xvii. 1), i.e. in	2061 B.C.
Abraham was one hundred and seventy-five when he died (Gen. xxv. 7) . .	1985 B.C.

Now it is a matter of common knowledge among Bible students that complications creep into these texts, to which reference has been made, if one goes outside the Old Testament. But the very significant fact remains that the original figures as they stand, and as set down in the Authorized Versions of Genesis and Exodus, work out as above. For they receive confirmation from an entirely independent source.

There is a sentence in one of the stories of Abraham which links his age to Ancient History. It runs as follows:

"And it came to pass in the days of Amraphel king of Shinar." (Gen. xiv. 1.)

This king Amraphel has long been identified with the great Babylonian monarch, Hammurabi. It is true that the identification has been disputed by some, but it has been generally accepted by British authorities for many years. One of the most recent opinions is that of Dr. Langdon, who writes:

"In my opinion Hammurabi, Ammarabi, etc., is Amraphel king of Kingin (Kinger, Singir, Heb Shinegar, Shinar (Gen. xiv. 9)), etc." (*Semitic Mythology*, p. 384).

The date of Hammurabi has now been ascertained by using the Science of Astronomy to interpret the archæological evidence. There are frequent references to dates on cuneiform tablets; the trouble, of course, has been to connect them to any precise period of our system of chronology. But among the many tablets some have been found that record the monthly heliacal risings and settings of the planet Venus. These appear to have been made for astrological purposes.

A series of them cover the twenty-one years of the reign of a certain king of Babylonia named Ammizaduga. The many attempts made to utilize this information for chronology will be found recorded in that monumental work, *The Venus Tablets of Ammizaduga*, by Langdon and Fotheringham (Oxford University Press). Here the fact can only be briefly recorded, that at long last, Dr. Fotheringham has been able to identify the period 1921–1901 B.C. as corresponding with the Venus records. This, then, represents the dates of Ammizaduga's reign. It was a piece of good fortune that the cuneiform tablets of the lists of kings already deciphered, enabled the authors to work out a clear succession of Babylonian kings between Hammurabi and Ammizaduga. With their aid, and working backwards, the following chronology is reached:

Ammizaduga	.	.	.	1901–1921 B.C.
Ammiditana .	.	.	.	1922–1958 B.C.
Abiešuh	.	.	.	1959–1986 B.C.
Samsuiluna	.	.	.	1987–2024 B.C.
Hammurabi .	.	.	.	2025–2067 B.C.

The whole chronology, from which the above is a brief extract, has been checked by the contract tablets which mention date harvest, or barley harvest, or attested thirtieth day of the month. It will thus be seen that Hammurabi reigned from 2067–2025 B.C. This period of time fits correctly into the chronology of the life of Abraham, as calculated from the Jericho dating. It is significant that astronomical work on this remote period proves the Jericho and Bible dating to be valid.

The movement of Terah and his family from Ur of the Chaldees to Haran, was a transfer from one seat of moon-worship to another; that is if Harran in the north of Assyria was the destination. And this seems appropriate in view of the Ras Shamra tablet, already referred to in this chapter, which mentions the moon-god Terach. Harran seems to have been a renowned seat of moon-worship where the moon-god was also known as Sin, and which in later times at least had a week of seven days.

But it has sometimes been contended that the real Haran, to which Terah took his family, was near Damascus, and was named after the son Haran who had died in Ur of the Chaldees. A place about fourteen miles from Damascus has been suggested, and even the Hauran, a district marked in our map to the east of the Sea of Galilee. If the ultimate destination of Terah's party was Canaan, there was no need whatever for him to migrate as far north as the more famous Haran. The association of Abraham with Damascus is referred to by Josephus in his *Antiquities* I, 7.2, written A.D. 93:

"And Nicolaus of Damascus in the fourth book in his history says thus—'Abram reigned at Damascus; being a foreigner who came with an army out of the land above Babylon called the land of the Chaldeans; but after a long time he got him up, and removed from that country also, with his people, and went into the land then called the land of Canaan. . . . Now the name of Abram is even still famous in the country of Damascus; and there is showed a village called from him the Habitation of Abram.'"

The Nicolaus here quoted was a well-known historian who wrote about a century earlier than Josephus. References have been found to the so-called Habitation of Abraham on inscriptions.

The situation of Haran further arises in connection with Jacob's flight from Laban (Gen. xxxi.). The patriarch travelling with his wives, his children and his cattle, could not possibly have covered three hundred and fifty miles in ten days. Yet that is the approximate distance from the northern Haran to Mount Gilead where Laban overtook his son-in-law. On the other hand, the distance from a Damascus Haran would only be about eighty-four miles, which fits the narrative.

The question raises far-reaching issues, involving the situation of Aram Naharaim (Aram of the two rivers) and Padan-Aram (the Plain of Aram). It has been pointed out that the literal rendering of Isaiah vii. 8 is: "The head of Aram is Damascus," and the two rivers, usually identified with the Euphrates and its tributary, may be the Abanah and Pharpar, the rivers of Damascus. If this should prove to be correct, other changes as revolutionary as those required by recent archæological discoveries must be made in commentaries of the Old Testament.

On consideration it would seem probable that the original destination of Terah and his family was Harran in Northern Mesopotamia, but that, later, they moved south near to Damascus, and named their new settlement Haran. Further on, when Abraham was in Southern Palestine, he sent his servant to his kindred in the north to obtain a wife for his son Isaac. The narrative reads as follows: "The servant arose and went to Mesopotamia, unto the city of Nahor." Now the original of the word translated "Mesopotamia" in our Bible is "Aram Naharaim," and the identity assumed creates confusion. The phrase "the city of Nahor" suggests a smaller place than the celebrated Harran in the north.

Another piece of evidence for the ultimate location of Abraham's relatives near Damascus in Syria is supplied by the name of Nahor's son—Laban. The two great ranges, or ridges of hills, in the interior of Syria are called Lebanon and Ante-Lebanon; and M. Dussaud, a distinguished French scholar, has drawn attention to the connection between the names Laban and Lebanon. The near relation of the Phœnicians to the Syrians and Hebrews has been already emphasized, and the interior of Syria, otherwise Aram, near Damascus, might well have seen a sojourn of Abraham, the Hebrew, and of Jacob, the Aramean. The Bible description of Abraham's departure into Canaan contains some significant passages which justify its reproduction here. It runs as follows:

"Now the Lord had said unto Abram, Get thee out of thy country, and from thy kindred, and from thy father's house, unto a land that I will shew thee: and I will make of thee a great nation, and I will bless thee, and make thy name great; and thou shalt be a blessing: and I will bless them that bless thee, and curse him that curseth thee: and in thee shall all the families of the earth be blessed. So Abram departed, as the Lord had spoken unto him; and Lot went with him: and Abram was seventy and five years old when he departed out of Haran. And Abram took Sarai his wife, and Lot his brother's son, and all their substance that they had gathered, and the souls that they had gotten in Haran; and they went forth to go into the land of Canaan; and into the land of Canaan they came.

And Abram passed through the land unto the place of Sichem, unto the plain of Moreh. And the Canaanite was then in the land. And the Lord appeared unto Abram, and said, Unto thy seed will I give this land: and there builded he an altar unto the Lord, who appeared unto him. And he removed from thence unto the mountain on the east of Beth-el, and pitched his tent, having Beth-el on the west, and Hai on the east: and there he builded an altar unto the Lord, and called upon the name of the Lord. And Abram journeyed, going on still toward the south."

(Gen. xii. 1–9.)

The call of Abraham described in the above verses, rings down all through the ages. It must have exercised a great influence upon those Anglo-Saxon pioneers who braved the dangers of the Atlantic Ocean, and carved out their civilization in the primeval forests of America.

There is evidence that Abraham's father, Terah, worshipped the moon-god, and we naturally wonder at what period in his life Abraham abandoned that type of worship. The Book of Jasher (to which reference has already been made) represents the patriarch as having done so while still at Ur of the Chaldees. But that would hardly account for the family leaving one centre of moon-worship for another centre of moon-worship.

Nevertheless Stephen, in his speech to the Jewish Sanhedrin before his martyrdom, says:

"The God of glory appeared unto our father Abraham when he was in Mesopotamia, before he dwelt in Charran." (Acts vii. 2.)

118

The phenomena associated with manifestations and messages from the Unseen, such as recorded here in Abraham's case, are only just beginning to be recognized by scientists. But there are some great names associated with the new science of Psychical Research, such as the late Lord Balfour, Sir William Crookes, Sir Oliver Lodge, Professor Hans Driesch, and others. Yet the tide of doubt still sets strong, swelled by the perversity of those who regard the radio as the only source and channel for æther communication.

But to return to archæology; it is interesting to notice how the pottery system of dating, adopted in the last few years, is verifying the antiquity of the places mentioned in the above quotation, and so testifying to the authenticity of the narrative. Thus Dr. Albright, the distinguished American archæologist, writes:

"Practically every town mentioned in the narratives of the Patriarchs was in existence in the Middle Bronze Age (2000–1600 B.C.). Examples are Shechem, Bethel, Ai, Jerusalem (Salem), Gerar, Dothan, Beersheba."

(The Archæology of Palestine and the Bible.)

A reference back to the chronology of Abraham as set out in the earlier part of this chapter, indicates that he entered Canaan about 2085 B.C., a date sufficiently near to the commencement of the Middle Bronze Age to justify the assertion that the towns mentioned in our quotation from Genesis xii., namely, Shechem, Bethel, and Ai, were then in existence.

The next incident in Abraham's life, on which recent exploration also supplies evidence, runs as follows:

"And Abram said unto Lot, Let there be no strife, I pray thee, between me and thee, and between my herdmen and thy herdmen; for we be brethren. Is not the whole land before thee? separate thyself, I pray thee, from me: if thou wilt take the left hand, then I will go to the right; or if thou take the right hand, then I will go to the left. And Lot lifted up his eyes, and beheld all the plain of Jordan, that it was well watered everywhere, before the Lord destroyed Sodom and Gomorrah, even as the garden of the Lord, like the land of Egypt, as thou comest unto Zoar. Then Lot chose him all the plain of Jordan; and Lot journeyed east: and they separated themselves the one from the other. Abram dwelled in the land of Canaan, and Lot dwelled in the cities of the plain, and pitched his tent toward Sodom. But the men of Sodom were wicked and sinners before the Lord exceedingly."

(Gen. xiii. 8–13.)

Those who have visited the Holy Land can readily picture Abraham and Lot standing on the great plateau of hills which tower above this Plain of Jordan on the western side, and looking down several thousand feet into the deep depression of what is now the Dead Sea. Reference has also been made to the fact that this Plain of Jordan lies far below sea-level, and was once very fertile. On this subject Dr. Albright has recently written:

"The results of this and numerous other expeditions made by the writer into the Jordan Valley, have definitely established the correctness of the very early Bible tradition that the valley was very prosperous and densely populated when Abraham came into the country."

And again even more emphatically:

"These researches, and those of Père Mallon and other scholars have proved that the most prosperous period of the history of this valley was in the Early Bronze Age (2500–2000 B.C.)."

To this may now be added the recent testimony of Professor Garstang regarding the earlier cities of ancient Jericho, to which reference has already been made. It will be seen from a glance at the map that Jericho stood at the northern end of what is now the Dead Sea; the cities of Sodom and Gomorrah may have been at the other end.

Soon after Lot and Abraham parted company, the raid on the cities of the plain by Chedorlaomer and his allies, already referred to in this chapter, must have occurred. The passage describing it runs as follows:

"And it came to pass in the days of Amraphel king of Shinar, Arioch king of Ellasar, Chedorlaomer king of Elam, and Tidal king of nations, that these made war with Bera king of Sodom, and with Birsha king of Gomorrah, Shinab king of Admah, and Shemeber king of Zeboiim, and the king of Bela which is Zoar. All these joined together in the vale of Siddim which is the salt sea. Twelve years they served Chedorlaomer, and in the thirteenth year they rebelled. And in the fourteenth year came Chedorlaomer, and the kings that were with him, and smote the Rephaims in Ashteroth Karnaim, and the Zuzims in Ham, and the Emims in Shaveh Kiriathaim, and the Horites in their mount Seir, unto El-paran, which is by the wilderness. And they returned, and came to Enmishpat which is Kadesh, and smote all the country of the Amalekites, and also the Amorites, that dwelt in Hazazon-tamar. And there went out the king of Sodom, and the king of Gomorrah, and the king of Admah, and the king of Zeboiim, and the king of Bela (the same is Zoar); and they joined battle with them in the vale of Siddim; . . . And the vale of Siddim was full of slimepits; and the kings of Sodom and Gomorrah fled, and they fell there, and they that remained fled to the mountain. And they took all the goods of Sodom and Gomorrah, and all their victuals, and went their way. And they took Lot, Abram's brother's son, who dwelt in Sodom, and his goods, and departed." (Gen. xiv. 1–12.)

The first sentence of this passage, "In the days of Amraphel king of Shinar," has already been discussed, and Amraphel identified with Hammurabi, the great Semitic legislator, whose code of laws, engraven on stone, was found some thirty years ago.

It will be seen that Chedorlaomer, the leader of the expedition, was king of Elam; and it is the culture of Elam which has been recognized by Sir Flinders Petrie in his excavations at Old Gaza.

The road by which the five kings invaded Southern Palestine was the old route through Transjordania. In *The Archæology of Palestine and the Bible*, Dr. Albright has some interesting notes on the places mentioned in the passage quoted above, thus:

Ashteroth Karnaim—"Formerly the writer considered this extraordinary line of march as being the best proof of the essentially legendary character of the narrative. In 1929, however, he discovered a line of Early and Middle Bronze Age mounds, some of great size, running down along the eastern edge of Gilead, between the

THE CODE OF LAWS OF HAMMURABI (AMRAPHEL, KING OF SHINAR)

Engraved on a stele of black diorite 8 feet high. This great Semitic conqueror reigned (2067–2025 B.C.) while Abraham was living in Canaan.

(*Musée du Louvre, Paris.*)

desert and the forests of Gilead. Moreover, the cities of Hauran (Bashan) with which the account of the campaign opens, Ashtaroth and Karnaim, were both occupied in this period, as shown by archæological examination of their sites."

Ham—"In 1929 Professor Jirku of Breslau and the writer undertook to investigate the antiquities of Ham, and immediately discovered the presence there of a small but very ancient mound, going back to the Bronze Age."

Mount Seir—"Some inkling of the reason which led the Eastern army down into the region of Seir, far south of the Dead Sea, may perhaps be obtained from the fact that there were extensive and important deposits of copper, manganese (used for kuhl) and other minerals in Seir and Midian."

This is all good evidence that the route taken by the four kings from the East accords with recent discoveries, since the dates assigned for Ashteroth and Karnaim—Early and Middle Bronze 2500–1600 B.C.— cover the period of Abraham.

The narrative relates how the battle with the five kings of the cities of the plain took place in the valley of Siddim, which is the Salt Sea, and which was full of slime pits. It is dangerous to speculate on the extent of the Dead Sea, obviously here referred to as "the Salt Sea," prior to the cataclysm which overwhelmed Sodom and Gomorrah. But extensive groups of salt sand mounds lie between the north end of the Dead Sea and Jericho. Professor Garstang has found ample evidence that Jericho had been a store city of the Hyksos. During the twelve years that Sodom and Gomorrah served Chedorlaomer, their tribute might well have been sent and stored there; and the battle in the Plain of Siddim might indeed have been fought among these mounds not far from its walls.

However that may have been, the defeat of the kings of Sodom and Gomorrah led to the carrying off of Abraham's nephew Lot. When the patriarch heard of it,—

"he led forth his trained servants born in his house, three hundred and eighteen, and pursued them unto Dan." (Gen. xiv. 14.)

There in the north near the Sea of Galilee, Abraham made a night attack on the army of the four Eastern kings returning home, and pursued them towards Damascus. The passage quoted is interesting, because Professor Yahuda has pointed out that the word translated "trained servants" is *hanakim*, an Egyptian word of about 2000 B.C. used for the retainers of Palestine chieftains.

On his way back, at a place called Shaveh (the king's vale), which may have been immediately below the ancient Jebusite city of Jerusalem, Abraham met an important and mysterious personage—Melchizedek king of Salem. During the years 1924–7 the author was associated with the Palestine Exploration Fund's excavations on the hill of Ophel, outside Jerusalem. The site is not far from the south-eastern end of the present wall. It was then used for the cultivation of cauliflowers.

The Fund had to compensate one grower to the extent of something like £300 for the loss of prospective cauliflowers on his patch! Beneath this "fertile" soil, were found the remains of the ancient Jebusite city of Jerusalem over which Melchizedek once ruled. In his days it was a small place of only about seven acres, surrounded by a wall twenty-four feet thick. It stood on the top of the ridge where the Kedron and the Tyropean valleys meet. To-day the Tyropean is nearly filled up with debris, and it is hard to realize what a stronghold Jebusite Jerusalem must have been.

Down underneath in the Kedron valley is the celebrated Virgin's Fountain, whence the villagers of Silwan, or Siloam, still draw their water. The well is fed by an intermittent spring which discharges its water thrice a day, apparently through a natural syphon in the rock. From the top of the ridge where once stood the interior of the city, there descends a subterranean passage, through which direct access to this Fountain was obtained by those inside the walls. Thirteen centuries after Abraham, the Jewish king Hezekiah was to cut the celebrated Siloam tunnel right through the ridge, so that the water from this Fountain flowed into the pool of Siloam inside his city's wall. But in far more primitive days the water was conveyed through narrow underground channels, hewn in the solid rock, along the side of the hill to the junction of the two valleys, and there used to irrigate the king's garden. It was probably here that Abraham and Melchizedek met, in beautiful surroundings, with the grim wall of the Jebusite Jerusalem towering above in the background.

"And Melchizedek, king of Salem, brought forth bread and wine; and he was the priest of the most high God," etc. (Gen. xiv. 18.)

The Hebrew words here translated "most high God" are "El Elyon." This is a very ancient title for the Deity. Sanchuniathon, the Phœnician sage, already quoted, says that Elioun was the principal deity of Gebal (Byblus), and that he was called Hypsistos—which is Greek for "Most High." An early inscription is also reported from elsewhere in which the name appears as "Elyan." The Semites, as will be noticed later, associated their worship of the Deity with the tops of hills or mountains. So Jerusalem was peculiarly fitted for the worship of God Most High. Concerning Melchizedek it is written elsewhere:

"Thou art a priest for ever after the order of Melchizedek." (Ps. cx. 4.)

And again the New Testament:

"For this Melchisedec, king of Salem, priest of the most high God, who met Abraham returning from the slaughter of the kings, and blessed him, to whom also Abraham gave a tenth part of all; first being by interpretation King of righteousness, and after that also King of Salem, which is King of peace; without father, without mother, without descent, having neither beginning of days nor end of life, but made like unto the Son of God; abideth a priest continually." (Heb. vii. 1–3.)

So it has been judged that Melchizedek was a very mysterious personage, and whole volumes have been written about him.

In considering religious problems created by the recently discovered Ras Shamra inscriptions, one acquires the impression that the writer of this Epistle to the Hebrews must have had some knowledge of Semitic religion before Moses. It is also remarkable that the formula "without father, without mother," etc., actually occurs on three of the Tel el Amarna tablets, written seven centuries after Melchizedek, by the then King of Jerusalem to the reigning Pharaoh.

The word Zedek was also a name identified with Jerusalem; for its king, whom Joshua fought in those Tel el Amarna times, was called Adoni-Zedek (Joshua x. 1). The word "Adoni" means "Lord," while "Melchi" corresponds to "King."

In the extracts from Sanchuniathon's writing there is a reference to one "Sydyc." It is suggested that Sydyc is the origin of Zedek. It may be that Melchizedek was a priest of the original monotheism, a survivor of the Shepherd King's aristocracy. The name is said to have been found in South Arabian inscriptions. But the passage quoted from the Epistle to the Hebrews suggests an even higher origin.

It is recorded in Genesis xvi. how Abraham's wife Sarah, because she bore him no children, gave him her maid Hagar, the Egyptian, as a kind of second wife. This procedure was in accordance with the legal code of Hammurabi (or Amraphel), to which reference has already been made. It is there laid down that the wife might give the husband a slave girl as a concubine to bear him children, but he must not then take one himself!

The same procedure was adopted later by both the wives of Jacob. Such incidents all testify to the genuineness of these stories. Hagar's son was named Ishmael and became the father of twelve nations. From the eldest, Nebaioth, sprung the Nabatheans, a race prominent in ancient history, and associated with the wonderful rock city of Petra. There is archæological evidence of the close association of these people with the Edomites, descendants of Nebaioth's first cousin Esau.

The final destruction of the cities of Sodom and Gomorrah by a cataclysm which, according to the chronology, took place about 2061 B.C., raises the question of their precise location, although no one seems to doubt the reality of the story. Controversy is still active as to whether the cities lay at the north or south end of what is now the Dead Sea. Dr. Albright thinks their ruins are submerged beneath the risen waters of the Dead Sea; and that five streams of fresh water which form oases at the south-east end are indications of them. On the hills at the south end are the ruins of a fortified High Place called Bab el Dra, and quantities of potsherds that indicate an occupation between 2600–1900 B.C. Near here evidence was obtained of Zoar, so the conclusion was reached that the waters of the Dead Sea had risen above their former level and submerged the ruins.

A recent pamphlet by Father E. Power, S.I., presents a strong case for the northern site. He opens his arguments with an impressive quotation from the Alexandrian Jew Philo (born 20 B.C.). After describing the iniquities of the Sodomites, Philo continues:

"He (God) suddenly orders the air, overcast with clouds, to pour down an abundant rain not of water but of fire. The dense flame rains down with a continuous and unceasing rush. Burnt are the fields and the meadows and the bushy groves and the luxuriant marsh-lands and the deep cattle-runs. Burnt is the plainland and all its produce of corn and other seed-crops. Burnt is the forest land on the hillsides, the trunks of the trees being consumed to the very roots. Cattle-pens and houses and fortifications and whatever the dwellings contained of public or private utility are all burnt together. The populous cities in a single day become the tomb of their inhabitants, the furniture of wood and stone becomes ashes and fine dust. When the flame had consumed everything that was visible above the earth it penetrated deep into the earth itself, which it burned, and destroyed the life-producing power therein existing, making it completely unproductive so that it might never again be at all able to bear fruit or grow grass. It still burns. The lightning flame is not extinguished but spreads or smoulders. The clearest evidence are the visible signs. The smoke which constantly ascends and sulphur which is dug out are a memorial of the past disaster. As a proof of the punishment inflicted by divine decree there remains a most evident demonstration of the ancient prosperity of the surrounding region, one of the neighbouring cities and the land round about it; the city is populous, the land is rich in fodder and corn and entirely fruitful."

The last sentence of this quotation clearly alludes to Roman Jericho of the time of Christ, to which references are made in a later chapter. It is remarkable how this fanciful description of what happened to Sodom and the other cities of the Plain, conveys a sense of reality to modern tourists standing on the Plain of Jordan, trying to locate, and to account for the cataclysm.

This interesting example of classical writing, from the pen of a man who lived in the time of Our Lord, has been quoted as evidence that the north end of the Dead Sea is the correct site of the cities of the Plain. More support for this view is obtained from studying Genesis xiii. 3 and 10. If, as is there suggested, Lot stood on the high ridge between Bethel and Ai when he looked down on the Plain of Jordan, he could not have looked down on the south end of the Dead Sea at all. These are powerful considerations, and should they prevail, archæological evidence concerning Sodom and Gomorrah is likely to be found soon.

The next incident in the life of Abraham concerns his sojourn at Gerar in South Palestine on which recent research has thrown some light. It is recorded in Genesis xx. But here it is necessary to point out that a precisely similar story is told of Abraham's son Isaac, in Genesis xxvi. If the Abraham story is in its proper place in the narrative, Sarah was an old woman when the incident happened, and it would almost seem as though there was a duplication of the narrative with that of Isaac and Rebekah. However this may be,

Sir Flinders Petrie's excavations at Gerar, in 1927, afford evidence in favour of one, or both stories. The narratives represent both Abraham and Isaac passing off their respective wives as their sisters, to Abimelech king of Gerar.

The Isaac story describes Abimelech as king of the Philistines, and the critics discredited the narrative on the ground that the Philistines had not come into Palestine at this early period of history. Petrie, however, found that the district round Gerar had been a great wheat-growing centre. The Philistines, or at least some of them, are said to have come from the island of Crete.

The excavations in recent years at Knossos, and other places in this island, have revealed the splendid civilization of Minos which goes back to those early times. But Crete was not a wheat-growing district; hence the presence of Cretan, or Philistine, representatives, in the wheat-growing country, behind the ancient seaport of Old Gaza, from whence the grain would be shipped to the island.

Another interesting confirmation of the Isaac story was noticed by Petrie when he excavated the palace, on the great Tell or mound of Gerar. Standing on the summit he observed that he could see directly into the tents on the Bedouin camping ground below the mound. In consequence of the fact that the wind nearly always blows in one direction in this district, the openings of these tents always face the palace; and doubtless have always done so. After Isaac had told Abimelech king of the Philistines that Rebekah was his sister, the story runs as follows:

"And it came to pass when he had been there a long time, that Abimelech king of the Philistines looked out at a window, and saw, and behold Isaac was sporting with Rebekah his wife, and Abimelech called Isaac and said, Behold of a surety she is thy wife."

(Gen. xxvi. 8.)

Abraham's sojourn at Gerar has brought about a reference to Old Gaza, the seaport whence the wheat was shipped to Crete. Abraham must have known all about this city, for at Gerar he was only eight miles away.

Old Gaza proves to have been the great seaport town of South Palestine many centuries before Abraham. Except for an allusion to the fact that the border of the ancient Canaanites extended from Zidon in the north, to Gaza in the south, the early narrative of the Old Testament is silent regarding it. The author recently motored down from Jerusalem to Old Gaza to visit its excavations. The route lay through Hebron, which appeared to be a good-size flourishing town. Then the road deteriorated, and many motorists had preferred the hard surface of the adjoining desert. There was a fair amount of grass, and one could picture Abraham's vast flocks in this big, open space. In the centre of Beersheba, a real country town, was a great well, said to have been the one dug by Abraham. And then into the desert again, now scarred by the remains of a Turkish railway, and many trenches and dugouts, all legacies of the Great War. Then through modern

Gaza, and civilization, and on south to Old Gaza (Tel el Ajjul)—fine old mounds on the north bank of a washout, which once must have been a wide river estuary. Why is there no reference to this large city in the sacred narrative? Abraham and his household had become a pastoral people: perhaps Gaza was too much like Ur of the Chaldees.

Whatever the reason, the history and civilization of Old Gaza (Tel el Ajjul) now being brought to light by Sir Flinders Petrie, seems quite as surprising as that of Ur of the Chaldees.

Scenes from the ruins of Pompeii in Italy must be familiar to our readers. The skeletons of streets and houses were disclosed intact, when the volcanic ashes with which Vesuvius covered them in A.D. 79, were cleared away. Old Gaza appears to have been deserted on account of the eruption of a plague, rather than that of a volcano; but the walls of its houses still stand eight feet high, the streets and doorways are completely preserved. Thus, one could pass through a city that reached its prime when Abraham lived eight miles away, but was abandoned ere Moses led Israel into the Wilderness, or the walls of Jericho fell. The plague that brought on this desolation is thought to have been spread by mosquitoes; and the half-dry channel of the river bed was still a breeding ground for quite a colony of these pests during the first season of the Petrie Expedition. Since that time the government has drained the swamp, and the excavators are saved this discomfort.

The houses of Old Gaza were three stories high; the ground-floor rooms had large square hearths for fires, stone jars stood in the corners, and the floors were stuccoed. At the entrance to some houses was a raised bench embedded with sea-shells, and a drain was made to carry off the water of ablutions.

The remains of a series of four or five palaces that have been superimposed upon each other have been excavated in this city. Even the earliest of these, which may date back as far as 3000 B.C., has a large bathroom 12 feet by 8 feet. The next palace above this first one had been built of yellow bricks, so well made that subsequent builders used them again. This, too, had a large bathroom and lavatory, white plastered, with underground stone drain. The third palace was built of mingled yellow and grey-black bricks in the time of Egypt's fifteenth dynasty (2371–2111 B.C.). A fourth palace, erected above all these, is ascribed by Sir Flinders to the sixteenth dynasty (2111–1593 B.C.): while finally, and above the four previous buildings, are the remains of the palace that played its part in the stormy times of the eighteenth dynasty of Egypt (1573 B.C. onwards), when the Shepherd Kings were finally expelled, and the Egyptians in turn attacked Palestine. All this vast civilization appears to have come first from the Semitic Babylonians, and later from the Shepherd Kings. And all the while ships from the coast of Phœnicia, such as were registered in the later Ras Shamra archives (1400–1360 B.C.), would be bringing wares or weapons, for peace or war, as the case might be, with Egypt. Such was the value of sea power even in these remote times.

Old Gaza was defended by a great sloping wall, or glacis, with a ditch, the mark of its Hyksos occupation. Two subterranean passages, each 500 feet long, one above the other, and leading out of the city, have also been found. They are very old, and seem to have belonged to the earlier cities, perhaps even to the very first. What was their purpose? They were wide and well made, perhaps for use by the city's garrison for counter-attack or for escape. Indications of passages inside the Hyksos rampart at Tell Duweir are referred to later, and a novel theory outlined as to their usage. The horse was used in sacrifices at Old Gaza, and the finds being made suggest that its inhabitants had such an abundance of gold ornaments that they were rather careless, and used to lose them in the mud of the streets, or else have them stolen. Reference has already been made to the Irish gold ornaments of 1500 B.C., but the find is so sensational that the mention of it bears repetition. There are also many highly finished fragments of pottery of types of unknown origin. This was to be expected at a Mediterranean seaport town of such importance and magnitude; but the existence of such a place in Palestine, and such a civilization there in the days of Abraham, and centuries before Abraham, is another piece of knowledge to be taken into account.

The birth of Isaac is associated with the long stay of Abraham at Beersheba; the memories of his residence there still seem to cling around that district. One does not feel that excavations are needed to find contemporary evidence of his sojourn in those parts.

There follows the strange chapter recording the attempted sacrifice of Isaac which opens with the words:

"And it came to pass after these things, that God did tempt Abraham, and said unto him, Abraham: and he said, Behold, here I am. And he said, Take now thy son, thine only son Isaac whom thou lovest, and get thee into the land of Moriah; and offer him there for a burnt offering upon one of the mountains which I will tell thee of."   (Gen. xxii. 1, 2.)

The events described in this chapter constitute an undoubted link between Semitic religion before Moses and the Crucifixion. Indeed evidence begins to suggest a far wider relationship to Christianity than Semitic religion.

The mountain in the land of Moriah was probably Mount Moriah. A thousand years later Solomon built his temple upon it. The Jerusalem of Abraham's days lay further away to the south-east. Abraham may have seen the spot when he visited Melchizedek. Even in David's days it was a threshing-floor.

Or the upper ridge, now called Mount Zion, may have been the scene of this event. It may even have been the site of the Crucifixion.

One further passage in the chapter calls for comment:

"And Abraham lifted up his eyes and looked, and behold behind him a ram caught in a thicket by his horns."   (Gen. xxii. 13.)

Among the ornaments found in the royal tombs of Ur of the Chaldees is one of a ram caught in a thicket. It has been pointed out at the commencement of this chapter that these ornaments were laid away in their tombs more than a thousand years before Abraham. Yet Abraham came from that same Ur of the Chaldees. Was the ram caught in a thicket, a symbol of some ritual ceremonial, which shaped itself into reality at Abraham's offering of Isaac?

At the death of his wife Sarah, Abraham purchased the Cave of Machpelah by Hebron for a burying-place for himself and his family from Ephron the Hittite. The record of the transaction resembles a cuneiform legal document in its phraseology:

"And the field of Ephron which was in Machpelah, which was before Mamre, the field and the cave which was therein, and all the trees that were in the field, that were in all the borders round about were made sure unto Abraham for a possession, etc."
(Gen. xxiii. 17, 18.)

The consideration was "four hundred shekels of silver current money with the merchants" (verse 16). This was probably money in the form of ingots, and not coined money. Previously we read that Abraham was very rich in cattle, in silver, and in gold (Gen. xiii. 2), all of which would be quite in keeping with the background of Abraham's days as revealed these last few years at Old Gaza. The presence of Hittites in South Palestine at this earlier period has already been referred to in a previous chapter. The Cave of Machpelah remains to this day, as one of the more sacred of the Mohammedan shrines. For Abraham is as great a man in the Moslem, as in the Christian, or Jewish faiths.[1]

The writer of these lines used as a lad to delight in Dean Stanley's account of his visit to this ancient shrine, with the late King Edward, then Prince of Wales. As an immense privilege the heir-apparent to the British throne was shown the splendid Mosque above the cave. In the cave itself, according to the Bible narrative, there rest the remains of Abraham, Isaac and Jacob with their wives, except Rachel. Jacob's body at any rate was embalmed in Egypt (Gen. 50-2, 3), and his mummy might yet be intact in Machpelah. There was also a tradition that the body of Joseph was taken there at a later period.

So matters remained until the Great War, and then in November 1917, in the course of Lord Allenby's advance on Jerusalem, Hebron was hurriedly evacuated by the Turks. It was then that Colonel Meinertzhagen, one of Lord Allenby's principal officers, actually entered the cave under the Mosque of Machpelah. Some accounts of the incident have already been published, but none can exceed in interest the following extract from his diary which Colonel Meinertzhagen has now most courteously supplied us. The document is the more valuable because it was written down within forty-eight hours of the event.

[1] "The Field of Abraham" is mentioned among the list of places which Shishak king of Egypt captured in the course of the conquest of Palestine about the year 920 B.C. Does this refer to the Field of the Cave of Machpelah?

THE INSCRIPTION OF SHISHAK, KING OF EGYPT
(940–919 B.C.)

It records the various places captured by him in the course of his invasion of
Palestine in the reign of Solomon's son, Rehoboam. The names include the
Field of Abraham.

EXTERNAL VIEW OF THE MOSQUE OVER THE CAVE OF MACHPELAH
NEAR HEBRON

Here Abraham, Isaac and Jacob were buried with their wives.

(*Courtesy of American Colony, Jerusalem.*)

EVIDENCE ABOUT ABRAHAM

Extract from Colonel Meinertzhagen's diary, dated from Rafa, Southern Palestine, on 28th November 1917:

"Motored through Beersheba and up the Jerusalem road to Hebron, my object being to try and get some sort of administration set up in this important centre immediately after our troops enter it. Our troops were holding a line just outside the town, but hearing that no enemy were within I went boldly into Hebron in my car and at once tried to find out where were the elders of the city. It was like a City of the Dead. I eventually got hold of a Jew and he told me all the city notables were hiding in the Mosque, so thither he conducted me but refused to pass beyond the entrance.

"I walked in and found the building apparently deserted. Passing up a passage in the massive building I entered a court and on the left was a mosque vulgarly decorated with the usual ornaments. It appeared to be only half furnished for I expect most of their good stuff had been hidden away. Finding nobody about I shouted out and, thinking I heard voices through an iron grid floor-door, I pulled it back and passed down a stone staircase into a chamber which was pitch-dark. Having only matches I could see little, but by lighting match after match I searched all round for people, finding nothing but a stone coffin with spiral columns at each corner, all in stone. I sat on the coffin, lit my pipe, but was soon driven out by the unventilated atmosphere. On emerging from the building I found my Jew awaiting me and he said I might find the notables in the house of the Kaimakam, so thither I repaired and there they were all expecting instant death."

As an additional detail, Colonel Meinertzhagen remembers that there were some men, including the

Mufti, in the underground chamber. They came out when called, but they did not include the men wanted.

When things became normal in Hebron an examination of the Mosque was made by experts, but the Moslem guardians, now returned under British protection, refused to allow anyone to again enter the cave. So matters are to-day; and whether the bodies of the patriarchs are yet there, still remains an open question.

Dean Stanley's account of the Mosque concluded (if the writer's memory be correct) with the following verses:

> "*What though the Patriarchs' Tombs be in the Valley,*
> *Though heathen hands have sealed the sacred caves,*
> *And the Red Prophet's children cry 'El Allee' [Allah]*
> *Over the Hebrews' graves!*
>
> "*Yet a day cometh when these white walls shaking,*
> *Shall bring again to life the living dead,*
> *And Abraham, Isaac, Jacob, reawakening,*
> *Spring from their rocky bed.*"

So let us leave Abraham and his immediate descendants. It is perhaps worth while to notice that Jacob el and Joseph el occur as place-names in a long inscription of Thotmes III among one hundred and nineteen places in Palestine which he claims to have captured about 1470 B.C. According to the chronology in this chapter, Jacob should have died in 1853 B.C., and Joseph survived him to perhaps about 1800 B.C.

The charming stories of Joseph and his brethren, which are some of the best that have ever been written (Genesis, chaps. 39 to 45), contain such an intimate knowledge of Egyptian life of this period, as illustrated for us on Egyptian monuments, that it is impossible to believe they were not committed to writing until some twelve hundred years afterwards!

To sum up then this chapter.—It is evident that the background supplied by recent excavations for the period of Abraham corroborates the sacred narrative. And further, that the Old Testament chronology is as correct as is the Bible geography. In the stories themselves confirmations occur even in detail; which are evidence that the narrative was written down at a very early date, when the memory of the events was still quite fresh.

X

THE EVIDENCE FROM JERICHO

EARLIER chapters of this work contain important references to the Jericho excavations. So it has become necessary to give an account of them without further delay and to cite the evidence from that source. But before taking this course, readers are reminded that nearly six centuries elapsed between the death of Abraham and the day when his descendants, under the leadership of Joshua, made their successful assault upon the walls of Jericho. During the latter part of that time, the Bible records many incidents in the life of Moses. A later chapter will revert to these stories; but even their significance depends upon the Jericho evidence, so it is expedient to set it down without delay.

Jericho, as will be seen on reference to the map, is just north of the Dead Sea, deep down below ordinary sea-level in the Jordan valley.

There may be those who will remember that, a year or two before the War, the Germans made extensive excavations at Jericho. It is a testimony to the skill of Professor Garstang that he has been able to disentangle from parts that were left undisturbed, the correct history of the city. The German work at

Jericho was very thorough and systematic; but it was carried out before the study of ancient pottery had reached a stage when it could be used for chronological purposes; and consequently the interpretation of what was found lacked the knowledge modern excavators have to guide them. The idea of reopening the excavation of the site of ancient Jericho arose in quite a roundabout sort of way.

Professor Garstang had some time earlier, in one of his journeyings through Palestine, discovered the ruins of the city of Hazor, far up in the north, about ten miles beyond the Lake of Galilee, in the direction of what is now known as Lake Huleh. So when the author joined forces, it was decided that the Professor should make a preliminary expedition to Hazor.

The site is a place now called El Kedah, and is one of the largest in Palestine, being about twelve hundred yards long and six hundred yards wide. It proved to be surrounded by great sloping ramparts of beaten earth, evidence of Hyksos occupation. On the south side the enclosure was dominated by the mound of a city rising one hundred and sixty-five feet above the neighbouring road.

So here was a good-sized city which Professor Garstang estimated might have contained a population of four thousand people, while the camp enclosure was large enough to accommodate thirty thousand men with a corresponding number of horses and chariots. Hazor thus appears to have been a typical example of the Shepherd Kings' system of offence and defence. Excavations revealed that the halcyon days of the city were about 1800 B.C., when this Hyksos power still flourished in Egypt. Then a great stone wall had encircled it besides the older fortifications. In consequence of its increase in population, the city had overflowed into the camp enclosure, so that houses had sprung up there as well, and made it the largest place in Southern Syria.

At the date subsequently ascribed to Joshua's invasion of Palestine, the town was not so prosperous, although the great natural strength and position remained; but it had been captured by Thotmes III in 1478 B.C., and had, to some extent, suffered from the overthrow of the Hyksos or Shepherd Kings. But it was still an important place, and remained a centre for horses and chariots. So we read of its king and his allies that:

"They went out, they and all their hosts with them, much people even as the sand that is upon the seashore in multitude with horses and chariots very many."

(Joshua xi. 4.)

The narrative goes on to recount the concentration of the allied kings, their fight with Joshua, and their subsequent defeat, and then continues:

"And Joshua at that time turned back, and took Hazor, and smote the king thereof with the sword: for Hazor before time was the head of all these kingdoms, and . . . he burned Hazor with fire . . . but as for the cities that stood still in their strength, Israel burned none of them save Hazor only; that did Joshua burn."

(Joshua xi. 10–14.)

Whoever wrote this part of the Book of Joshua seems emphatic that Joshua burned Hazor, since he twice affirms it. That reiteration may have exasperated modern commentators; for they have been equally emphatic that Joshua did nothing of the sort! Despite the lapse of more than three thousand years, they were able from their arm-chairs to detect the fact that the destruction of Hazor must be referred to the incidents connected with Sisera and Deborah, recorded in the fourth chapter of Judges.

So now there was demonstrated the value of excavation and pottery dating to settle the dispute on the spot. Professor Garstang found that the pottery evidence pointed to the fact that the city had been destroyed by fire about the middle of the late Bronze Age (1400 B.C.), long before the date assigned to Deborah by commentators and critics. Could this, then, be the destruction recorded in the Book of Joshua? The answer to that question appears to be suggested by one of the Tel el Amarna letters written about 1380 B.C. by the Egyptian envoy in the north of Palestine to the reigning Pharaoh. He writes:

"Let my lord the king recall what Hazor and its king have already had to endure."

After Hazor, Professor Garstang decided to seek further evidences of date for the Joshua campaigns, so he went to South Palestine in search of it.

Bible students will remember that the capture and destruction of Ai took place after the Fall of Jericho.

It is recorded with considerable detail in the eighth chapter of the Book of Joshua. The description of the ambush by which Ai was captured involved references to the surrounding country. The writer of the sacred narrative has been so clear, and so accurate, that a modern tourist when visiting the site, can readily identify the spot where the ambush was laid, where Joshua attacked, and how it all happened. This geographical evidence weighs strongly in favour of the authenticity of the narrative, and to its having been committed to writing at about the time it all happened. Critical endeavours to reconcile this accuracy with their theories are painstaking but grotesque. Only two other brief allusions to the account need concern us:

"And so it was, that all that fell that day, both of men and women, were twelve thousand, even all the men of Ai . . . and Joshua burnt Ai and made it an heap for ever, even a desolation unto this day."

(Joshua viii. 25, 28.)

When Jericho is described, surprise may be expressed at the smallness of the place. Ai was a larger city than Jericho, and yet its inhabitants only numbered 12,000. The site of Ai seems never to have been reoccupied; it has literally remained a desolation to this day. Professor Garstang, on his arrival from the north, proceeded to dig into this heap of ruins. He soon found ample evidence of destruction by fire; and the potsherds, like those of Hazor, belonged to the middle of the late Bronze Age. There was nothing later than 1400 B.C.

146

After this further discovery it was natural that the Professor should decide to reopen the excavations of Jericho, the first—and, to Bible readers, the most famous city—taken by Joshua. The ensuing pages of this book tell of the results gleaned from four later expeditions to Jericho. But readers may like to know now that potsherds found there, in this preliminary dig, told the same tale as those of Hazor and of Ai.

Here, then, were three ruined cities, Hazor, Ai and Jericho, all destroyed by fire about 1400 B.C.; and in reverse order, all stated in the Bible to have been captured and burnt by Joshua.

This evidence for the correctness of the Book of Joshua was, however, overshadowed by the fact that the potsherds supplied a date of about 1400 B.C. There never had been any unanimity among Bible authorities regarding the date of the Exodus. But there has been a considerable consensus of opinion during the past generation, that it must have taken place about 1220 B.C. So, allowing for the forty years' wandering of the Israelites in the Wilderness, Jericho should have been captured and burnt about 1180 B.C. Yet, here the potsherds were recording an earlier date by over two centuries! Admitting that the pottery dating was only approximate, and might not be exact to within five-and-twenty years, an approximation of 220 years was quite another story.

Thus, on Professor Garstang's return to England, the subject was considered in all its bearings, and it was decided that further and fuller excavations at Jericho would be likely to furnish the key to the puzzle; so the following winter Professor Garstang and his staff returned to resume work there.

Here it may be helpful to insert a few geographical and historical details about Jericho for the benefit of readers who have not visited Palestine.

Modern Jericho is situated on the western side of the Plain of Jordan, near to where that river enters the Dead Sea. The site of ancient Jericho, the scene of four more years' excavation, lies half a mile farther away from the river towards the mountains which roll up to the Promised Land far above.

The Jericho that is so often mentioned in the New Testament was the Roman city of that name; and it occupied a site rather above and outside modern Jericho, on the road that afterwards enters the mountain passes and leads to Jerusalem. According to Josephus the Roman Jericho must have been a delightful winter resort, shaded by palm-trees. He writes as follows:

"There are in it many sorts of palm-trees different from each other in taste and name; the better sort of them when they are pressed, yield an excellent kind of honey, not much inferior in sweetness to other honey. This country withal produces honey from bees; it also bears that balsam which is the most precious of all the fruits in that place, cypress trees also, and those that bear myrobalanum; so that he who should pronounce this place to be divine, would not be mistaken, wherein is such plenty of trees produced as are very rare, and of the most excellent sort. . . .

"In summer time this country is then so sadly burnt

148

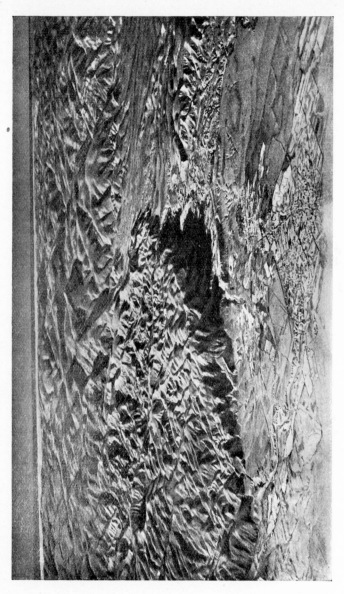

AERIAL PHOTOGRAPH OF THE JORDAN VALLEY

Showing modern Jericho in the foreground, the ruins of ancient Jericho behind it in the neighbourhood of the hills. In the far distant background can be seen the Mediterranean, and the centre of the picture gives some idea of the hilly character of the whole country.

(Courtesy of "The Times.")

up that nobody cares to come to it . . . as in winter again it becomes warm, and if you go into it, it appears very gentle. The ambient air is here also of so good a temperature that the people of the country are clothed in linen only, even when snow covers the rest of Judæa."

(Josephus—Wars Book, 4–8–3.)

Roman Jericho was also distinguished by the winter palace of Herod the Great, and a Hippodrome. Josephus records the fact that Herod himself died at his Jericho palace, and so saved the lives of the most illustrious of his Jewish subjects, whom he was planning to massacre in the Hippodrome. So much for the Roman Jericho, the city associated with the ministry of Jesus Christ—ruined mounds, and the remains of aqueducts, still testify to its existence. The quotation from Philo, concerning the destruction of the cities of the Plain, in the chapter on Abraham, undoubtedly refers to it.

The site of the original Jericho, more remote from the river on the sandy plain, was no doubt chosen for the sake of the adjoining springs of Ain-el-Sultan and Ain-el-Duk. To the tourist the ruins appear to be an egg-shaped cluster of sand mounds. The city that stood here when the Israelites approached the Jordan from its eastern side, barred the route to the western plateau. It also controlled the only copious supply of pure water on the western side of the Jordan for something like twenty-five miles. Jericho was thus the gateway to the Promised Land.

In an earlier chapter reference is made to the fact

that in the East it was customary to rebuild cities time after time on the same site, the ruins of the previous city being levelled and used for the foundations of the next one. This was done on the site of the original Jericho.

Professor Garstang has provisionally dated the earliest occupation from 2500–2100 B.C. That city's single wall consisted of large clay slabs banded with thick layers of bituminous earth, after a Babylonian fashion. The next city above it belonged to the Middle Bronze Age pottery period. Its wall was some ten feet thick, and built of large grey bricks; it has been traced round three sides of the city. On the east side near the spring it was supported by a tower, parts of which still remain, then some sixty feet high. Evidence in its strata is again apparent of Babylonian culture and influence, and the explorer assigns a date of 2100–1900 B.C. to it, but Petrie's dating would probably place it much earlier. The third city, according to an Egyptian scarab of the thirteenth dynasty, included the Hyksos period. The city then covered the whole mound, which was entirely surrounded by a stone glacis crowned with a brick parapet at occupation level, and further protected by an outer ditch. The area thus enclosed was about twelve acres, and included the spring. This expansion marked the greatest cultural and material prosperity of the place. This city was destroyed, and its ramparts dismantled at the close of the Hyksos period, probably by the avenging Pharaohs. Its successor, built on the same site in the late Bronze

Age (1600–1200 B.C.) forms the subject of this narrative. Those who desire further details of the earlier occupations are referred to Professor Garstang's book, *The Foundations of Bible History—Joshua, Judges* (Constable & Co.).

Traces of a still later occupation are also in evidence, but it was of a partial character. Bible students will remember that after his destruction, Joshua put a curse on the site:

"Cursed be the man before the Lord that riseth up and buildeth this city Jericho; he shall lay the foundation thereof in his firstborn, and in his youngest son shall he set up the gates of it." (Joshua vi. 26.)

This curse was fulfilled in the time of Ahab king of Israel, for it is recorded that:

"In his days did Hiel the Bethelite build Jericho; he laid the foundations thereof in Abiram his firstborn, and set up the gates in the loss of his youngest son Segub." (1 Kings xvi. 34.)

The evidence left of this occupation cannot be assigned to an earlier date than about 900 B.C., which would correspond to the time indicated in the Bible narrative. Thus a period of over five centuries appears to have elapsed before this attempt was made, and its disastrous consequences probably caused the final abandonment of the site. What afterwards became the site of Roman Jericho may have succeeded it.

Such was the outward appearance of the remains of ancient Jericho—such was the lie of the surrounding land.

The early part of each of the succeeding years of 1930, 1931, 1932 and 1933 found Professor Garstang, with some hundred and more workers, engaged in digging into these sand-covered ruins. It will be seen that the results obtained carry consequences and conclusions of far-reaching importance. It is not usual for archæological work to tell a complete story. As a general rule the information gleaned is too fragmentary to be appreciated by the general public. Many more excavations in other places are needed to piece the fragments together. But here in the mounds of ancient Jericho the evidence was complete.

The examination of potsherds dug out of the debris of the city was on a much more extensive and systematic scale than on the preliminary expedition in 1929. So great was the importance of verifying the date of the destruction that, in 1930, Professor Garstang and his wife cleaned and examined no fewer than sixty thousand fragments from the strata of the burned city. At the expedition in the following year (1931) another forty thousand fragments were treated in a similar manner. They all attested to the same date, that of the middle of the late Bronze Age (1400 B.C.), before the infiltration of the Mykenean ware.

In the preceding chapter reference has been made to the very generally accepted belief that the Exodus had taken place more than two centuries later than the date supplied by the potsherds. It is not easy for authorities on any subject to change their views on important questions; and rather than do so in the present instance, the system of pottery dating, at least so far as Jericho was concerned, was called in question.

It was fortunate, therefore, that in the course of the 1931 expedition another discovery was made, which enabled the excavators to check the date of the potsherds taken from the debris of the burnt city. Professor Garstang then succeeded in finding the necropolis, or cemetery, where the inhabitants of Jericho had buried their dead from the earliest times. The site lay between the city mounds and the western hills, in the neighbourhood of a small valley that leads down to the north end of the ruins. Covered over and concealed by the sand of the plain, the tombs had escaped the notice of countless generations of plunderers, and their contents lay intact.

In 1932 they yielded a rich hoard of fifteen hundred unbroken pottery vessels of all periods of the Bronze Ages. Mingled with them were bronze weapons and trinkets, such as bead necklaces of carnelian, shell, and bone, and a number of bone flutes. There was also a human headed vase of a quite uncanny character. But, far more important than all, was the presence in some of the richer tombs of scarabs inscribed with the royal cartouche of the reigning Pharaoh. These scarabs, eighty in all, served to date the pottery in their particular tombs, which in turn could be compared with the broken ones found in the burnt city.

As the opening of tombs proceeded, it was found that the later dated ones were farther away from the city. Special attention was therefore paid to them in order to find the latest interments. In due course a number of tombs were opened that proved to belong to the century 1500–1400 B.C. and included the royal tombs of the period. There were found a succession of eighty scarabs bearing the cartouches of the Hyksos and eighteenth dynasty Pharaohs. In one was uncarthed scarabs bearing the joint names of Princess Hatshepsut and Thotmes III (1501–1487 B.C.) and in another two royal seals of Amenhetep II (1413–1377 B.C.). As the series of dated scarabs all come to an end with the two royal seals of Amenhetep III, there is evidence, quite independent of the pottery, that the city also ceased to exist during that period. For the two centuries that followed there were no interments; the very distinctive pottery and decoration of the time of Akhenaten and Tutankhamen was not represented at all. Thus everything pointed to the reign of Amenhetep III (1413–1377 B.C.) as marking the period when Jericho fell. Efforts to obtain an even closer approximation are made in a later chapter.

XI

JERICHO'S WALLS AND INTERIOR— THEIR TESTIMONY

THE walls of Jericho! Does anything else from the Old Testament so linger in the memories of our childhood? The old picture Bibles contained wonderful illustrations of gigantic walls, toppling over, as Joshua and the priests, in full vestments, with trumpeters blowing, encircled them in their march. Let us see to what extent reality confirms all these conceptions.

The excavations revealed the fact that the walls themselves did, on the whole, justify such pictures. They consisted of two parallel walls built of sun-dried bricks. The outer wall was six feet thick, and the inner one about double that width. Both appear to have been about thirty feet high, with a fifteen feet space between them.

Careful examinations disclosed the fact that these formidable defences must have been somewhat faulty in construction. The bricks were sun-dried and contained no binding straw. Some of them were as much as twenty-two inches in length, while others were much smaller. And though all were about four inches thick, still the variations made it difficult to keep uniformity in the courses; so there were differences of level, and occasional gaps. These were filled up with mud mortar, but the work appears to have left much to be desired.

Again, the foundations consisted of several layers of stones gathered from the neighbourhood, which were also of different sizes, and were not evenly laid. Besides all this, both walls suffered from faulty foundations, the inner one having been built to overhang the remains of a much earlier wall, partly in ruins; and the outer one on debris at the very edge of the mound on which the city stood. In reading the fuller and more technical description of Professor Garstang, one is inclined to wonder if the expression "jerry built" was originally "Jericho built." Across or astride these great parallel walls, houses had, in places, been built, which thus linked them together. These ties may have been regarded as a source of strength, but as eventualities turned out they proved a source of weakness.

The second chapter of the Book of Joshua tells how Joshua sent two spies into Jericho, and how the two came into the house of an harlot whose name was Rahab. Here, in justice to Rahab, it should be said that the word "harlot" in this context perhaps only means an innkeeper. This woman afterwards appears to have married Salmon, the father of Boaz, who in turn married Ruth the Moabitess. Rahab figures in the royal genealogy (Matt. i. 5) as one of the ancestresses of King David. However that may be, we read in Joshua ii. 15 that "her house was upon the town wall, and she dwelt upon the wall."

We now come to an aspect of ancient Jericho where the excavations do not confirm the conceptions of our youth. Though the walls themselves, at least to outward appearance, were so formidable, the area they enclosed only measures seven acres. The whole circumference of the city was about six hundred and fifty yards. Our disappointment is somewhat modified by the fact that the Jebusite Jerusalem which David captured, and which the Palestine Exploration Fund excavated in 1925-6-7, was about the same size. Schliemann experienced a like disillusionment in 1873 when he excavated the city of Troy which Homer tells us so long withstood the Grecian hosts. Indeed, it would almost seem that these ancient cities were more in the nature of places of refuge resorted to on the approach of an enemy. Under peaceful conditions a large proportion of the inhabitants of Jericho would dwell outside the walls under the palm-trees to the east of the city. In early times these groves of palms appear to have made the Plain of Jordan a much more acceptable place of residence than it is to-day; and allusion has already been made to the deterioration of climate since the time of Abraham.

But to return to the walls of Jericho. How came these formidable defences to collapse at the sound of Joshua's trumpets? The Press reports of the excavations brought the author quite a number of letters from those who had their pet theories to account for the phenomena. At one time Professor Garstang himself was inclined, with some reservation, to the idea that the wall might have been undermined; and that timber, used to hold up the foundations, was fired when the Israelites on the seventh day commenced to encompass the city seven times. In his book the Professor gives a certain amount of prominence to this theory; but in a postscript at the end (p. 404), he adds that the 1931 investigations pointed to an earthquake as the cause of the catastrophe.

The 1932 and 1933 excavations have completely exploded the theory of a pious fraud on the part of Joshua. The walls *had fallen outwards quite flat* in various places, particularly on the west side of the city which alone had remained undisturbed by the German excavators. In 1932 a thorough examination of the outer wall disclosed the fact that it had either slipped, or been pushed, over the brink of the slope on which it stood. The debris, on the surface which had suggested possible undermining, was cleared away. It was then found that the striations of the natural soil both under the foundations, and under the surface on which the walls fell, were unbroken and undisturbed from below; but that these lines had been deflected downwards by the great weight of the walls falling on the surface above.

The unsatisfactory character of the foundations on which the walls stood, and the defective nature of the brickwork as revealed in portions of the walls still standing, no doubt contributed to the catastrophe; while the fact that the walls were tied together by the houses built astride them, linked them in a simultaneous downfall.

Reference has already been made to the Great Rift, far below sea-level, running through Palestine from north to south, and terminating in the Plain of Jordan and the Dead Sea. The tremors of the great earthquake which shook the country in 1927 ran across this Rift from east to west. The buildings inside the burnt city, as well as the walls, bear evidence of a similar great upheaval.

The phenomena that facilitated the crossing of the Jordan by the Israelites give further support to the idea of earthquakes. We are told that when the procession of Israelites, headed by the priests, reached the eastern side of the river then in flood, and so impassable:

"The waters which came down from above stood and rose up in one heap, a great way off at Adam, the city that is beside Zarethan." (Joshua iii. 16.)

The site of the city Adam is the modern El Damieh, some sixteen miles above Jericho. Opposite El Damieh, on the other side of the river, is a place called Zarthan, which is undoubtedly the Zarethan mentioned in the above text. There the Jordan flows rapidly through forty-feet-high clay banks, which even in normal times are subject to landslides. During the earthquakes of 1927, these banks collapsed, and so dammed the river that no water flowed down for more than twenty-one hours. Here then is a repetition of the phenomena described in the text quoted above, and that in our own time, and associated with seismic disturbances.

That earthquakes were associated with Joshua's

crossing of Jordan is also suggested by the following passage:

"When Israel went forth out of Egypt, the house of Jacob from a people of strange language; Judah became his sanctuary, and Israel his dominion. The sea saw it and fled; Jordan was driven back. *The mountains skipped like rams, and the little hills like lambs.* . . . *Tremble thou earth*, at the presence of the Lord."

(Ps. cxiv. 1–7.)

Elsewhere we read:

"Lord when thou wentest forth out of Seir, when thou marchedst out of the field of Edom, the *earth trembled* . . ." (Judges v. 4.)

There is a popular impression that when incidents like the drying up of Jordan and the fall of Jericho's walls can be traced to "natural causes," there is an end of the miracle. Such a belief is surely a superficial one. Science now openly confesses that we know little or nothing of the nature of natural causes; they may very well, therefore, be due to the action of the Deity. Indeed, the position to-day appears to be that, while the Bible represents God as working through "natural causes," leading scientists now affirm that simple actions of everyday life partake of the nature of miracles. If the Jordan was dried up at the moment when Israel reached its brim, if the walls of Jericho fell just when the trumpets sounded, these "coincidences" testify to the direct action of the Deity although working through natural causes.

So much, then, for the walls of Jericho! So completely did they fall flat outwards in places, that a clear path was opened for the invaders:

"The wall fell down flat, so that the people went up into the city every man straight before him, and they took the city." (Joshua vi. 20.)

Let us see what Professor Garstang found inside the city as a result of his excavations in 1930, 1931, 1932 and 1933.

As in the case of other cities of the period, the ingress and egress from Jericho seems to have been of a restricted character. The narrative of the visit of the spies conveys the impression that Jericho had but one gateway:

"It came to pass about the time of the shutting of the gate, when it was dark . . . and as soon as they which pursued after them were gone out, they shut the gate." (Joshua ii. 5 and 7.)

The excavations that have been made suggest that the assumption of a single gateway is correct. None has been found in the walls that have been uncovered either on the west, north or south sides of the city. On the other hand, a gate tower has been unearthed on the east side adjacent to the springs of water.

It is an imposing edifice, no less than fifty-four feet long and twenty-four feet wide, remarkably well built of grey brick. Though it shows traces of being one of the oldest buildings in the city, yet its ruins still stand more than sixteen feet high. They contain three deep store chambers extending right down into the foundations. Within the city the ground slopes directly upward from the gate tower to a great building on the mound called spring hill, which is believed to be the remains of the royal palace. This edifice seems to have been built round a quadrangular open space. It was explored in 1932 and 1933, and proved to date back to 2000 B.C. or earlier. The palace area overlooked the spring. The main building, of which little more than its foundations and drainage system remained, stood in the centre of the city on the high ground, and had a regular hive of sixty store-rooms extending down the slope. The Hyksos scarabs, or seals found in this area, testified to its occupation by the Shepherd Kings. It was obvious that this was once a Hyksos depot of more than local importance. The inhabitants of the city in Joshua's time had used these store-rooms again, and their contents will be described in due course. Here in the debris on the slope was found the only cuneiform tablet that was discovered. The writing is of the same style as that on the Tel el Amarna tablets, and the language appears to belong to Northern Syria, but the characters were too fragmentary to allow of decipherment. In the uppermost layers of the store-rooms of the palace and the area of destruction, were several hundred fragments of painted pottery vases, such as were found intact in the neighbouring tombs, in addition to the Cypro - Phœnician ware. Expert opinion assigns to these distinctive wares a date between 1600–1400 B.C. Similar specimens from the tombs in a more perfect condition were found, together with

A RECONSTRUCTION OF THE JERICHO OF JOSHUA'S TIME

From a painting made on the site by Miss M. Ratcliffe, after the excavations in 1932.

royal Egyptian scarabs, so their date cannot be in doubt.

At the north-west end of the city stood the great citadel, or migdol, whose walls in places still rise to a height of nearly forty feet. They had very substantial foundations, and appear to have suffered least from the earthquake which overthrew the neighbouring walls.

It may be conjectured that Rahab's house, or inn, was astride the walls not far from this building; for after the spies had been let down by her with the aid of a cord passed through a window, they escaped unseen to the neighbouring western hills. We may further deduce from the narrative that Rahab's house did not share the destruction that came from the falling of the walls, since she and her relatives were saved alive (Joshua vi. 25). The proximity of the citadel certainly appears to have held up the walls in the neighbourhood.

A good example of critical methods and conclusions may be quoted in connection with this incident:

"The wall fell down flat is mere literary hyperbole intended to convey the completeness of the victory; and probably nobody would be more amazed than the actual writer to learn that his words were ever required as a point of faith to be understood literally. . . . Had the walls collapsed entirely Rahab and her household could not have escaped." (*The New Commentary*, p. 194.)

It is, of course, straining the sense of the Book of Joshua to infer that the wall fell down flat outwards *entirely* all round the city; but that does not justify the description of the incident as "a mere literary hyperbole." Professor Garstang's discoveries about the walls, as detailed, prove it was nothing of the sort.

But to return to the interior of Jericho: the excavations revealed that the houses of the city were small and clustered together in oriental fashion. Their contents furnished ample evidence that the city had been taken at a time when its inhabitants were pursuing the usual vocations of daily life.

The further fact was revealed that Jericho had been most systematically burnt, although it had not first been systematically plundered. There, in the houses, were found foodstuffs, such as wheat, barley, lentils, onions, dates and pieces of dough, all reduced to charcoal by the intense heat of the conflagration, and so preserved for more than three thousand years—mute witnesses to the course of events attending the destruction of Jericho. Why had these foodstuffs been left untouched and uneaten by their captors? The sacred narrative furnishes the answer to the inquiry:

"The city shall be devoted, even it and all that is therein, to Jehovah." (Joshua vi. 17; Revised Version.)

The Authorized Version has: "The city shall be accursed," etc., which does not bring out the full sense of the Hebrew original. The expression "devoted to the Lord," signifies "set apart for sacrifice." Then we read:

"And ye in any wise keep yourselves from the devoted thing, lest when ye have devoted it, ye take of the devoted thing; so should ye make the camp of Israel accursed, and trouble it . . ." (Joshua vi. 18.)

Hence it is manifest why the foodstuffs were untouched, and their subsequent fate is also described:

"And they burnt the city with fire, and all that was therein." (Joshua vi. 24.)

Professor Garstang was impressed with the extent of the conflagration, and the thickness of the burnt strata enveloping the ruins, so he came to the conclusion that Joshua and his men, after the capture, systematically collected wood and other combustible material from all round the district, to make one huge bonfire of the "devoted" city.

Reference has already been made to the interior of the palace. There was found ample confirmation of the evidence supplied by the interior of the houses. To quote Professor Garstang's own words:

"Every room in the palace area tells the same tale of walls half fallen, reddened by fire amid layers of white ashes and masses of charcoal, rising through and above the ruins. The store-rooms were filled with great pottery vessels ranged in rows, and, though now crushed to fragments and their contents burnt, some of them may be seen to have been filled with grain and other food-stuffs, while some were sealed up and still show the dregs of their once fluid contents.

"In and among the debris of these great store vessels are found the remains of smaller vases which, apparently protected by the others, have in some cases partially escaped destruction. Twenty-six have been found in a single room. They correspond with the objects taken from the dated tombs, and they will give us that decisive evidence which we came to seek as to the date of the final overthrow of the Bronze Age city."

Later he wrote:

"Now we were able to compare whole jars and vases piece by piece from those of the dated tombs. They all proved to be types of the fifteenth century B.C., not a single specimen was found in the palace rooms which could be assigned to the familiar period of Akhenaten (1377–1361 B.C.)."

An analysis of the contents of the tombs gave parallel results. The pottery series includes plentifully the painted wares, and Cypro-Phœnician imports, distinctive of late Bronze Age 1, but only eight vessels that might be assigned independently to a later date than 1400 B.C. An examination of the scarabs is conclusive; to the number of one hundred and sixty-five, they range continuously through the Hyksos period and early eighteenth dynasty of Egypt. They comprised the Egyptian royal names Hatshepsut and Thotmes III, to the reign of Amenhetep III, when the series comes to an abrupt end. Let us turn now to the chronology based on such convincing evidence, and compare it further with other dates of the period.

XII

THE DATE OF THE EXODUS

THE reasons which have prompted many scholars to conclude that the Exodus took place after the death of Rameses II, 1229 B.C., are due to the mention of that name in Genesis and Exodus. Thus it is written:

"And Joseph placed his father and his brethren, and gave them a possession in the land of Egypt, in the best of the land, in the land of Rameses as Pharaoh had commanded." (Gen. xlvii. 11.)

Here the passage, taken as it stands, would lead us to believe that Joseph lived in the days of Rameses. This is, of course, contrary altogether to the Bible narrative, which represents the Israelites as being four hundred and thirty years in Egypt. Joseph lived at the commencement of that period, while Moses lived at the end. Here then is evidence that the expression "the land of Rameses" was a description given to a district of Egypt at a much later date. The next passage which bears upon the subject reads:

"And they [the Israelites] built for Pharaoh treasure cities, Pithom and Raamses." (Exod. i. 11.)

Further on it is stated that after the Exodus:

"The children of Israel journeyed from Rameses to Succoth." (Exod. xii. 37.)

If the word "Rameses" is used in the first text quoted in this chapter, for a district which was not so named till over four hundred years later, it is reasonable to consider whether this place Rameses may not also have been so called at a later date. The original name for New York was New Amsterdam, yet later writers, although dealing with events which occurred when it was New Amsterdam, would still call it New York. Here in England the Roman name for York was Eboracum, but later writers would use the name York.

A further consideration is the suggestion in *The Speaker's Commentary*, that Rameses may have been an old name dating from the reign of Aohmes I, the founder of the eighteenth dynasty (see below). Efforts to locate the cities of Pithom and Rameses have all been unsatisfactory, so far as throwing any clear light on the problem. For Rameses II was a notorious appropriator of the work of past generations, and habitually erased the names of his predecessors and inserted his own.

The element of uncertainty which has in the past hung round the date of the Exodus, does not seem to have been shared by the Egyptian chronology of the corresponding period. Rightly or wrongly, Egyptologists are fairly well agreed regarding the dates of the Pharaohs of the eighteenth and nineteenth dynasties. The following list is compiled from Sir Flinders Petrie's article in *Ancient Egypt* (March 1931) entitled "A Revision of History."

EIGHTEENTH DYNASTY

Aohmes I	1573–1560 B.C.
Amenhetep I . . .	1560–1539 B.C.
Thotmes I	1539–1514 B.C.
Thotmes II	1514–1501 B.C.
Thotmes III	1501–1447 B.C.
Amenhetep II . . .	1447–1423 B.C.
Thotmes IV	1423–1413 B.C.
Amenhetep III . . .	1413–1377 B.C.
Akhenaten	1377–1361 B.C.

Those who have just finished reading the preceding chapter, will remember that Jericho was destroyed in the reign of Amenhetep III, the last but one on this list. The evidence of date supplied by the pottery fragments on the burnt site, has been checked by similar but unbroken pottery vessels, which are in turn dated by the Egyptian scarabs found side by side with them in the necropolis. Of equal importance is the fact that the series of scarabs of the earlier Pharaohs of Egypt, from the Hyksos down through the eighteenth dynasty, all come to an abrupt end with two of this Amenhetep III.

The scarab evidence seems extremely hard to dispute —if Jericho was destroyed say half a century earlier, how came Amenhetep III scarabs in the tombs? If two centuries later, what has become of all later scarabs? Unless further evidence should come to light, the reign of Amenhetep III (1413–1377) constitutes a reliable basis from which to calculate the date of the Exodus. Since we know that after the Exodus Israel wandered forty years in the Wilderness before the capture of Jericho, we have only to add forty to both the beginning and end of Amenhetep's reign, to obtain a correct interval of time within which the Exodus should have taken place.

It will be noticed that the interval thus obtained (1453–1417) falls within the reigns of several Pharaohs. Can we find any evidence which will give a closer approximation? The Book of Exodus furnishes a clue for, after describing Moses' flight from Egypt and sojourn in Midian, it goes on to narrate:

"And it came to pass in the course of those many days that the king of Egypt died." (Exod. ii. 23.)

After this statement the incident of the Burning Bush is described; to be followed by the return of Moses to Egypt, the ten plagues and the Exodus.

A reference to the Egyptian chronology set down on the previous page indicates that three kings of Egypt died between 1453 and 1417. They were:

Thotmes III in 1447, Amenhetep II in 1423, and Thotmes IV in 1413.

But the verse quoted above suggests that the king who died had reigned for a long time, and that he was the king from whom Moses had fled. According to other passages in the Bible, Moses had been absent from Egypt about forty years (Acts vii. 30). These two considerations lead to the identification of Thotmes

III as the king in whose reign Moses fled from Egypt; and this monarch's long reign of fifty-four years (1501–1447) more than satisfies the forty years of Moses' absence. The Exodus must, therefore, have taken place after Thotmes III's death in 1447 B.C. and during the reign of Amenhetep II.

Calculations based on the Jericho excavations can now for the moment be set aside, and reference made to Bible chronology. The dates at the head of the margins in the Authorized Version of the Bible, only represent the calculations of Archbishop Usher, and are no part of the original Bible. It is essential, therefore, to refer direct to the Bible text. Next to the Exodus from Egypt, the greatest event in Old Testament history was the founding of Solomon's Temple at Jerusalem. The interval that elapsed between these two most important events should therefore have been correctly transmitted and correctly recorded in the following verse:

"And it came to pass in the four hundred and eightieth year after the children of Israel were come out of Egypt, in the fourth year of Solomon's reign over Israel . . . that he began to build the house of the Lord." (1 Kings vi. 1.)

The date of the foundation of Solomon's Temple might be known to the Freemasons, whose ritual is said to be associated with the building of it. But information from that source seems unavailable; either members do not know, or they are not prepared to say.

The Cambridge Ancient History places the accession of

Solomon at 970 B.C.; Sir Flinders Petrie in a recent article in *Ancient Egypt* fixes it at 960 B.C. All recent evidence seems to point to these dates as a correct approximation, and on that basis Solomon's fourth year would be either 967 or 957 B.C. It seems fair then to take a margin of dates between them as likely to be correct for the founding of the Temple. And it is interesting to notice that computations from data supplied by the Jewish historian Josephus, justify these figures. When the 480 years are added to them, some interval between 1447 and 1437 B.C. is suggested for the date of the Exodus. But the dates postulated by the archæological evidence fall between 1447 B.C. and 1417 B.C., and the latter is quite an extreme outside limit.

This very remarkable agreement with the Jericho discoveries carries a great deal of conviction that the figures must be correct.

For if the forty years' wandering in the Wilderness is deducted from this Bible chronology (1447–1437), Jericho fell between 1407 and 1397. Since Amenhetep III began his reign in 1413, either of these dates would allow sufficient time for two of his scarabs to be buried in Jericho's necropolis. Thus, so far as can be judged from the knowledge gleaned in the last ten years, the date of the Exodus has now been definitely ascertained.

Preference will perhaps be given to the later date, *i.e.* 1397 B.C. for Jericho's fall, both because it allows another ten years of Amenhetep III's reign for the burial of the scarabs, and also because it appears more nearly to link up with the assumed dating of the Tel el Amarna letters referred to in a later chapter.

One of the "assured results" evolved through the incorrect assumption that the Exodus took place in 1220, and that Joshua and his men entered Canaan in 1180, has already been cited in the Introduction. It cast doubts on the bulk of the Israelites ever having been in Egypt at all! Other distortions of the Bible narrative are due to the same initial mistake. It is a testimony to the correctness of our Jericho dating that it preserves the integrity of the sacred text. Whereas, before, critics were entangled in a mass of confusions and contradictions, which were used to discredit the Pentateuch, as well as the Book of Joshua, these disappear in the light of the correct dates.

As a number of devout Bible students have placed the Exodus at 1487 B.C. it seems expedient to examine this earlier date with the evidence before us.

The date is reached by interpreting 1 Kings vi. 1 to mean 480 years from the entry into Canaan, and making the "going out of Egypt" to represent the forty years in the Wilderness.

The Septuagint, or Greek Version of the Old Testament, translated from the original Hebrew into Greek about 300 B.C., reads:

"And it came to pass in the four hundred and fortieth year after the departure of the children of Israel out of Egypt. . . ."

This suggests that the 480 years of our Authorized Version includes the time in the Wilderness, while the Septuagint date does actually run from the entry into Canaan. That would make the two agree. But to make the 480 years run from the entry into Canaan, and so place the Exodus at 1487, and the Fall of Jericho at 1447, violates both Egyptian chronology and the record of the Jericho scarabs. Unless the Egyptian chronology of this period, which is at present generally accepted, is quite wrong, the year 1487 B.C. was the fourteenth year of Thotmes III's reign, while he was still associated on the throne with the Princess Hatshepsut. Who then was the king of Egypt whose death brought Moses' return from Midian? It could only have been Thotmes II who deceased fourteen years earlier. That would involve an interval of fourteen years for Moses to return from Midian to Egypt, which seems altogether too long. While, since Thotmes II only reigned thirteen years, the interval between when Moses fled from Egypt and the death of the king is altogether too short. In that case, also, the Princess Hatshepsut, deduced in the next chapter as Moses' patron, was in reality his bitter enemy.

But the 1487 date becomes even more impossible to maintain against the evidence of Jericho's scarabs. If Jericho fell in 1447 there should have been an entire absence of the scarabs of the succeeding kings—Amenhetep II, Thotmes IV and Amenhetep III in its necropolis. The presence of these is fatal to the theory, unless, of course, there is a mistake in chronology and all these Pharaohs really reigned before 1447 B.C. A possible contingency, but for this period of Egyptian chronology an improbable one.

The Egyptian historian Manetho, quoted though he be somewhat scornfully by Josephus, yet places the Exodus of the Israelites in the reign of a certain king Amenophis. Our own Egyptian authorities, from certain other indications of this monarch, have long identified him with Amenhetep II, in whose reign, according to the Jericho calculations, the Exodus took place.

At the time of going to press an article has appeared in the *Illustrated London News*, by Dr. Nelson Glueck of the Hebrew Union College, Cincinnati, entitled "King Solomon's Copper Mines." It refers to expeditions made in the earlier half of 1934, under his leadership, in Transjordania, as far south as the Gulf of Akaba. The article contains the following:

"The Exodus of the Israelites through Southern Transjordania could not have taken place before the thirteenth century B.C."

This statement attempts to revive what is known as the late date theory, which places the Exodus in the days of the Pharaoh Mernepthah, after the death of Rameses II. On that account the evidence in support of the above assertion deserves examination. Dr. Glueck and his friends claim that they found no evidence of Edomite occupation of Edom before the thirteenth century B.C., and he directs attention to the twentieth chapter of Numbers where the Israelites in their wanderings through the Wilderness were refused a passage through Edom. (Num. xx. 21.)

Dr. Glueck's evidence is inconclusive and unsatisfactory for the following reasons: If any reliance is to be placed on the Book of Genesis, the Edomites were the descendants of Esau; their pedigree is given at great length in Genesis xxxvi. Esau lived before the Israelite sojourn of four hundred and thirty years in Egypt. Even though that period of time were halved, as some have suggested, and even though the Exodus took place in 1220 B.C., nevertheless the Edomites would be in Transjordania as early as 1470 B.C. Yet Dr. Glueck finds no traces of them! The reply might be that the Edomites were probably a nomadic tribe like the Bedouin in their early days, and that the Bedouin leave no pottery evidence. But that raises the question *when* did the Edomites cease to be a nomadic tribe, and so settle down, that the pottery system of dating could be applied to testify to their existence?

Further consideration of this subject makes it clear that it is an abuse of this system of dating to attempt to use it in this manner. Fragments of pottery scattered over a country are but poor indications of *the arrival* of a people. They cannot carry anything like the same conviction that concentrated layers of pottery do in a burnt city like Jericho, for dating that city's destruction. Dr. Glueck's evidence testifies that the Edomites, or some people thought to be them, were settled in their country in the thirteenth century B.C. But it is straining evidence of this character to affirm that they could not have been there at an earlier date.

As a matter of fact there is now entirely independent evidence for the presence of the Edomites in their country when Israel desired to pass through it.

A Ras Shamra tablet mentions Edom associated with the tribes of Zebulon and Asher. The French authorities agree that these are allusions to the Israelite tribes, and they date these tablets between 1400–1360 B.C.

XIII

THE LIFE OF MOSES

THE remarkable agreement between the Jericho pottery and scarabs, and the chronology both of the Bible and of the Egyptian kings, justifies us in endeavouring to ascertain whether further light can be cast upon the Bible narrative by combining it with Egyptian history. It may be objected that in taking this course we shall be passing out of the region of solid fact into that of conjecture. Yet it is conjecture justified by the facts to an extent that does not require an exercise of the credulity so generously accorded to past critical theories.

Moses was one hundred and twenty years of age at his death immediately before Joshua captured Jericho about 1400 B.C. (Deut. xxxi. 2). Moses was therefore born about 1520 B.C. As he was about forty years old when he fled from Egypt (Acts vii. 23 and 29), he left that country about 1480 B.C. Now in Egyptian history the period (1520–1480 B.C.) is the very period when the great Princess Hatshepsut dominated that country. It will be seen on reference to the chronology of the eighteenth dynasty set out in the previous chapter, that this period includes the last six years of the reign of Thotmes I, the whole of the reign of Thotmes II,

THE PRINCESS HATSHEPSUT
(1537–1485 B.C.)

The most celebrated woman in Egyptian history. She was the daughter of
Thotmes I. According to chronology she must have been the daughter of
Pharaoh who found Moses floating in the ark of bulrushes on the Nile. Josephus
says this lady was named "Thermuthis," which confirms this identification.

(*Courtesy of the Metropolitan Museum of Art, New York.*)

and the first part of the reign of Thotmes III. Readers are reminded that scarabs bearing the joint names of Hatshepsut and Thotmes III have actually been found at Jericho.

Hatshepsut was the only surviving daughter of Thotmes I, and his Queen Aahmes or Ahmose. Her mother was a daughter of Amenhetep I, and was of royal blood by both parents. Thus Hatshepsut had a unique claim to the throne, of which only her sex debarred her from taking full advantage. Neither her father, nor Thotmes II, nor Thotmes III possessed such qualifications; they all had mothers who were of inferior rank. Hatshepsut, on the other hand, was the descendant of the old Theban princes, who had fought and expelled the Shepherd Kings, and there appears to have been a strong party in Egypt who regarded the blood of this line as alone entitled to royal honours. Her father Thotmes I seems to have tried to secure her direct succession; anyhow, she is said to have taken a leading part in the government of Egypt before the reign of Thotmes II. Now both our chronology, and the unique career of this remarkable woman, suggest that she was the daughter of Pharaoh who found Moses in the ark of bulrushes afloat on the Nile (Exod. ii. 5). The Jewish historian Josephus tells about events in the life of Moses not recorded in the Book of Exodus: in particular he recounts incidents which actually fit in with the activities of Hatshepsut far up the Nile. Josephus represents Moses as commanding an Egyptian army, and besieging the city of Meroe near the junction of the Blue and White Nile. Against this may be placed the fact that in his *Antiquities of the Jews,* and in his controversy *contra Apion,* he seems to contradict himself as to the length of time the Israelites were in Egypt, and the precise date of the Exodus. He does, however, mention the name of the princess who found Moses in the ark of bulrushes. He says it was "Thermuthis," in which we see an echo of the name Thotmes, or Tahutmes, which was borne by each of the three Pharaohs in whose reigns Hatshepsut played such a leading part. Again what has been said about her royal descent, and what is known besides of the lady's history, are quite in harmony with the statement that she was ready to recognize Moses as her son (Heb. xi. 24). And it is also remarkable that the time of her death so closely coincides with the flight of Moses from Egypt to Midian. If Moses had been Hatshepsut's favourite, he had little mercy to expect from Thotmes III. For, after her death, this Pharaoh so detested her memory that he destroyed or defaced her monuments.

Nor do coincidences seem to end with the death of Hatshepsut and Moses' flight to Midian. The further career of Thotmes III has also a considerable bearing upon the Old Testament narrative.

From previous chapters it will be understood that Palestine and Syria were well known to the Semitic invaders of Egypt, and consequently to the Semitic Pharaohs or Hyksos Kings as long as they ruled that country. But this country of Canaan, promised to Abraham and his descendants, seems to have been little known to the native Egyptians, until their own Pharaohs of the eighteenth dynasty drove out the Hyksos, and in turn invaded and conquered it. The stream of migration had been all the other way; the Hyksos and their predecessors the Semitic Babylonians, had come into Egypt from the north for generations. It was those Pharaohs, whose names and dates figure at the commencement of the previous chapter, that made expeditions into Palestine and through it to Syria. This was all long after Joseph had ruled in Egypt, and the Israelites had been settled in the land of Goshen.

It is recorded that Amenhetep I (1560–1539) raided all Syria, and so did his successor Thotmes I (1539–1514), who even crossed the Euphrates. But during the supremacy of the Princess Hatshepsut (1520–1487), Egyptian attention appears to have been directed southwards rather than northwards. As already indicated, we read of expeditions up the Nile, and of fleets of ships that went by sea to Central Africa. In a later chapter reference is also made to Hatshepsut's activities in the Peninsula of Sinai.

But after her death Thotmes III commenced, and carried out, a systematic series of invasions and conquests of Palestine and Syria, such as no Pharaoh before or after ever achieved. He made seventeen great expeditions into these countries, captured the cities, and broke down their defences.

The accounts of these campaigns, engraven in Egyptian hieroglyphics on temple walls and monuments, are reproduced by modern writers of ancient history.

We read, for example, a detailed narrative of Thotmes III's great battle at Megiddo in North Palestine. On a grander scale, it reminds us of Joshua's surprise attack on Ai, referred to in an earlier chapter. And there at Megiddo, Thotmes captured nine hundred chariots, two thousand two hundred horses, two hundred suits of armour, and so on. Certainly the chariots and horses are reminiscent of the Shepherd Kings' occupation. Less than a century later, hard by Megiddo, it is recorded in the Bible that Joshua put to flight the Northern Confederation of Kings "with chariots and horses very many."

When we read these Egyptian records of Thotmes III, the question forces itself upon us—Why did commentators assume that Moses never wrote down his records? For Moses was *actually living* in Midian *at the very time* all these seventeen campaigns were fought and recorded on monuments.

"And Moses was learned in all the wisdom of Egypt." (Acts vii. 22.)

So it has become preposterous to affirm that all Moses said and did, was handed down by oral tradition for eight centuries. After Thotmes III's death, and the Exodus in the reign of Amenhetep II, this later Pharaoh, as well as Thotmes IV, pursued to some extent the same policy of conquest and subjugation of Palestine and Syria. That would be during the forty years while Israel was in the Wilderness.

Can we connect all this with the Bible narrative?

THOTMES III
(1501–1447 B.C.)

The Pharaoh of the Oppression, and the greatest conqueror in Egyptian history. What is called "Cleopatra's Needle," now on the Thames Embankment, is actually one of his monuments.

(Photo—Cairo Museum.)

Here was Canaan, a land then intensely cultivated with vines and olive-trees, oaks and fig-trees on the hillsides, and cornfields and pastures in the valleys; but a country defended by a multitude of cities, small, it is true, but with very formidable defences and warlike inhabitants. These had, however, notoriously been weakened, and even destroyed, in the campaigns of Thotmes III. It was Moses' opportunity, immediately after the Exodus, to lead the Israelites into the land promised to their forefathers. He proposed to do so, and sent twelve spies as a preliminary for that purpose. These brought back the following report:

"We came unto the land whither thou sentest us; and surely it floweth with milk and honey; . . . nevertheless the people be strong that dwell in the land, and the cities are walled and very great."

(Num. xiii. 27, 28.)

This report so discouraged the Israelites that they neglected the opportunity, and were condemned to wander many years more in the Wilderness. Meanwhile, Amenhetep II and Thotmes IV continued the work of destruction, and so reduced the fighting force of Canaan, that its inhabitants became dependent upon the power of their suzerain Egypt.

Is there anything in the Pentateuch, or the Book of Joshua, to justify the supposition that these attacks of Egypt paved the way for Israel's conquest of Canaan? There are three remarkable passages:

"I will send *my terror* before thee . . . and I will send *hornets* before thee which shall drive out the Hivite, the Canaanite and the Hittite from before thee. I will not drive them out from before thee in one year: lest the land become desolate . . . by little and little I will drive them out before thee." (Exod. xxiii. 27–30.)

A second reference to this mysterious insect the hornet is made later:

"Moreover the Lord thy God will send *the hornet* among them until they that are left and hide themselves, perish from before thee." (Deut. vii. 20.)

And again after the conquest Joshua reminds the people:

"And I sent *the hornet* before you which drave them out from before you, even the two kings of the Amorites: but not with thy sword, nor with thy bow."
(Joshua xxiv. 12.)

Professor Garstang's book contains the illuminating reminder that *the Hornet was the badge of Thotmes III and his successors*. This figurative allusion to the power of Egypt, will be seen later to furnish an explanation of the perplexities which arise when the narrative of Israel's sojourn in Palestine is considered, as recorded in the Book of Judges.

The story of Moses' sojourn in the land of Midian is an important one. The cause of his flight there from Egypt, when about forty years of age, is set out as follows:

"He [Moses] spied an Egyptian smiting an Hebrew, one of his brethren. And he looked this way, and that way, and when he saw that there was no man, he slew the Egyptian, and hid him in the sand. And when he

went out the second day, behold, two men of the
Hebrews strove together: and he said to him that did
the wrong, Wherefore smitest thou thy fellow? And
he said, Who made thee a prince and a judge over us?
intendest thou to kill me as thou killedst the Egyptian?
And Moses feared and said, Surely the thing is known.
Now when Pharaoh heard this thing, he sought to slay
Moses. But Moses fled from the face of Pharaoh, and
dwelt in the land of Midian: and he sat down by a
well. Now the priest of Midian had seven daughters:
and they came and drew water, and filled the troughs
to water their father's flock. And the shepherds came
and drove them away: but Moses stood up and helped
them, and watered their flock. And when they came
to Reuel their father, he said, How is it that ye are
come so soon to-day? And they said, An Egyptian
delivered us out of the hand of the shepherds, and also
drew water enough for us, and watered the flock. And
he said unto his daughters, And where is he? Why is
it that ye have left the man? call him that he may eat
bread. And Moses was content to dwell with the man:
and he gave Moses Zipporah his daughter."

(Exod. ii. 11–21.)

A few verses later Reuel is called Jethro, so he has
been accredited with the double name Reuel Jethro.
According to the Bible Moses spent forty years in
Midian, and something ought to be learned about the
country. Midian was the name of one of Abraham's
sons by Keturah (Gen. xxv. 1–2), and the land takes
its name from him. Closely associated with the
Midianites were the Ishmaelites, also descended from
Abraham, through Hagar the Egyptian.

The earliest mention both of Midianites and Ishmaelites occurs in the story of Joseph and his brethren. After he had been put in the pit:

"There passed by Midianites merchantmen; and they drew and lifted up Joseph out of the pit, and sold him to the Ishmaelites for twenty pieces of silver."

(Gen. xxxvii. 28.)

The title of "merchantmen" associates the Midianites with trade, probably in this case between Syria, Egypt, and the Red Sea.

The location of the country of Midian has been already described in our chapter on geography. There are traditions there of Moses' residence. As long ago as the days of the Crusades, one writer says: "Near Madyan is the well and at it a rock which Moses uprooted." This Madyan lies inland about two-thirds of the way down the Gulf of Akaba.

In the year 1877, the celebrated traveller, Sir Richard Burton, went on an expedition to Midian on behalf of the Khedive of Egypt. His quest was for a gold mine, but the samples of mineral which he brought back for analysis in Cairo, did not appear to have contained enough gold to encourage further efforts. However, Burton made a second expedition to the country and a summary of his report will interest our readers. He wrote in *The Land of Midian* (Pref. xxiv.):

"We who have travelled through a country like Midian finding everywhere extensive works for metallurgy; barrages and aqueducts, cisterns and tanks; furnaces, fire brick, and scoriæ; open mines and huge scatters of spalled quartz; with the remains of some eighteen cities and towns—we cannot but form a different and far higher idea of its mineral capabilities than those who determine them by simple inspection of a few samples."

The analysis of the samples Burton brought back indicated that the land contained copper in the north, and apparently gold in the south, and also abundance of iron ore. The whole country is extremely wild and rocky, and the interior is still but little known. The quantities of smelting furnaces along the coast suggest that the gold from Ophir, wherever Ophir may have been, was brought up the Red Sea in ships, and then smelted, and brought overland. There is a record of this traffic in the days of King Solomon, in which the Phœnicians also participated. For information about that we refer our readers to 1 Kings ix. 26–28; 1 Kings x. 11–14; or 2 Chronicles viii. 17, etc.

Dr. Glueck, whose expedition to the district of Transjordania, and down to the Gulf of Aquaba in the early part of 1934, has already been referred to, found ample evidence of copper mines worked in the days of King Solomon. He suggests that some of the copper was used to pay for the gold from Ophir. There is no doubt that long before the days of Solomon this land of Midian was a great mining centre. And there is evidence that the miners also worked other mines in the Peninsula of Sinai opposite. These people were all of Semitic origin, whether descended from Abraham, as the Midianites, or from South Arabia, the adjacent country. We shall read more about them and their religious beliefs in the next chapter. Some have located the scene of the Book of Job in Midian. Certainly the writer, traditionally said to be Moses, was well acquainted with mining, for we read:

"Surely there is a mine for the silver, and a place for gold which they refine. Iron is taken out of the earth, and copper is molten out of the stone. Man setteth an end to darkness, and searcheth out, to the furthest bound. The stones of obscurity [turquoises?] and thick darkness. He breaketh open a shaft away from where men sojourn; they are forgotten of the foot; they hang afar from men, they swing to and fro. As for the earth, out of it cometh bread: and underneath it is turned up as it were fire. The stones thereof are the place of sapphires [turquoises?] and it hath dust of gold. . . . But where shall wisdom be found?"

(Job xxviii. 1-12; Revised Version.)

It was somewhere in the interior of this country, away from the immediate vicinity of mines and smelting furnaces, that Moses lived for forty years keeping sheep for his father-in-law Jethro. Unlike our English shepherds, the Eastern ones do not drive their sheep but lead them. So Moses one day led his flock to the back of the Wilderness, and came to the mountain of God unto Horeb. Some confusion has been created by a misunderstanding of the meaning of the expression "mountain of God." The association of the tops of hills or mountains with worship, and with communion with the Deity, was a characteristic feature of the ancient Semitic religion. Reference has already been made to Abraham's projected sacrifice of Isaac on

Mount Moriah. The description of the dramatic scene on the top of Mount Carmel when Elijah confronted the prophets of Baal contains the statement that:

"He repaired the altar of the Lord that was thrown down." (1 Kings xviii. 30.)

So even here in the north of Palestine, far from Jerusalem, is another testimony to the general use of the tops of mountains for worship.

Thus the confusion which has arisen between Mount Sinai in the Sinaitic Peninsula, and Mount Horeb in Midian, on the other side of the Gulf of Akaba. Both were "mountains of God"; that is to say both were spots associated with burnt offerings, and worship to the Deity; and possibly also with appearances or manifestations from the Unseen. In the case of Moses in Midian, the manifestation took the form of the Burning Bush, to which reference will be made in a later chapter. Moses' long sojourn in Midian was ended by this incident, and he returned to Egypt to call the new Pharaoh to account, and to demand in God's name the release of God's people. During this long residence in Midian, Moses must have had constant contact with primitive Semitic customs, and ceremonies and ritual, even if he had not already learned and practised them in Sinai, as will be suggested in the next chapter.

The visit that Jethro, the priest of Midian, afterwards paid Moses, and the proposal he made for the appointment of officials to relieve Moses in the work of government (Exod. xviii.) have led to the suggestion that in matters of ceremonial Moses was also indebted to him. But Moses would be also familiar with the splendid ceremonies and vestments of Egypt.

During the last few years it has been suggested that the wanderings of the Israelites in the Wilderness occurred in the interior of this land of Midian. That notion has more to be said for it than the wild idea that the wanderings referred to a migration right across Asia! But Sir Flinders Petrie who explored the Peninsula of Sinai, has pointed out that the geographical details indicated in the Bible apply there; and that if it was not the actual scene of the wanderings, some later writer must have adapted the narrative to suit Sinai. In view of the striking confirmation of the Sacred Narrative in the case of the Fall of Jericho, we are hardly entitled to assume that elsewhere such changes have been made. In the course of these wanderings in the Wilderness, when the Israelites had come out of the Peninsula of Sinai, and had reached Shittim on the opposite side of the Jordan to Jericho, a Midianitish woman brought a bitter punishment upon her people. The battle between the Israelites and the Midianites is recorded in Numbers xxxi. At a later date this nation also became the instrument of an oppression from which Gideon delivered Israel (Judges vi.). As for Hobab, the son of Jethro, Moses' father-in-law, he seems to have accepted Moses' invitation to throw in his lot with the Israelites (Num. x. 29–32). From a reference to him again (Judges iv. 11) we gather that his descendants were called Kenites (see also Judges i. 16), possibly smiths, or workers in metal.

XIV

THE EVIDENCE FROM SINAI

THE Jericho dating has already enabled us to trace connections between the Bible narrative and Egyptian history—between Hatshepsut, the Egyptian princess, and Moses, the Semitic leader, who after her death led the Israelites into Sinai. In the light of archæology this connection increases in interest.

As long ago as 1904–5 Sir Flinders Petrie led an expedition into the Peninsula of Sinai, the Wilderness where Israel wandered for the forty years before Jericho was taken. Right in the middle of these barren wastes, on one of the hills, Sir Flinders examined and explored a very ancient temple and shrine called the Temple of Serabit. This sanctuary was associated with the neighbouring turquoise mines; it contained a shrine dedicated to Hathor, the "Mistress of Turquoise." The researches revealed the fact that the Egyptian kings had, from remote times, interested themselves in the mines, and had intermittently organized expeditions to work them. Across the Gulf of Akaba in the land of Midian, as stated in the last chapter, there is ample evidence of mining on a large scale. The Peninsula of Sinai has probably always been nominally Egyptian territory. But it was a remote

191

spot for Egypt. The comparative proximity of Midian, and the mining propensities of its inhabitants, evidences of which remain, both on the Sinai shore of the Gulf of Akaba, as well as on the Midianite side, suggest that the workers in these turquoise mines were Midianites. The reference quoted in the last chapter from the Book of Job seems peculiarly applicable to these turquoise mines. Anyhow, this Temple of Serabit in Sinai had been used for a form of worship quite unlike that practised in Egypt.

The name Hathor itself carries no religious significance, since it was used by the Egyptians as a general title for strange goddesses. The type of worship carried on at this temple was associated with burnt sacrifices. The immense heaps of ashes, still remaining, testified all the more to ritual observed, because the rocky site is bare of all trees; and the wood must have been carried up at least one thousand feet from the plain below.

Hill temples, like that of Serabit, are unknown in Egypt, while burnt offerings on High Places are equally foreign to the worship of that country. On the other hand, the system was a distinguishing feature of the Semitic religion from the remotest times, as was incidentally noticed in the last chapter in connection with Mount Horeb. There seems, then, no doubt that the men who worked these mines, even if they were not actually Midianites, belonged to that Semitic race, of which the Israelites were an important part.

Another feature of the ritual practised at this temple

in Sinai, were the many small stone altars for burning incense. The Egyptians, on the other hand, always burnt incense in a metal shovel. In Exodus xxx. 1 we read: "And thou shalt make an altar to burn incense upon." An elaborate system of ablutions must have been associated with the ritual of this Temple of Serabit, for Sir Flinders Petrie found four successive great lavers or tanks. Here, again, we are reminded of the Temple worship:

"Thou shalt make a laver of brass to wash withal, and thou shalt put it between the tent of meeting and the altar, and thou shalt put water therein. And Aaron and his sons shall wash their hands and feet thereat." (Exod. xxx. 18, 19.)

Or, again, we recall the ten lavers that stood in Solomon's Temple. (1 Kings vii. 38.)

Another feature of Serabit is the number of standing stones associated with sleeping shelters. These monoliths have been set up obviously for religious purposes. They are of a type unknown in Egypt. Again we are reminded of Jacob's dream, and his subsequent action:

"And Jacob . . . took the stone that he had put for his pillows and set it up for a pillar, and poured oil upon the top of it." (Gen. xxviii. 18.)

There were other peculiarities of these Semitic miners who worshipped at the Temple of Serabit. They knew how to keep accounts, and *they had a system of alphabetical writing*. Besides Egyptian monuments with their characteristic hieroglyphics, there were mysterious signs cut on sphinxes and the like. Alas! Some vandals had smashed up many of these invaluable evidences, but the scraps that remained have received a great deal of attention from scholars during the past thirty years. An illustration of this writing on a sphinx is given opposite.

The key to the riddle of reading these inscriptions appears to have been found by Mr. Alan H. Gardiner. In a Quarterly Statement of the Palestine Exploration Fund in 1929, he suggested that certain signs represented the word "Balat." This clue was followed up by Professor Martin Sprengling of the University of Chicago, who claims to have deciphered the inscriptions. The readings largely refer to votive offerings to Balat. One within a mine on the rock is read: "I am the miner Shamilat, foreman of mineshaft No. 4."

Professor Sprengling thinks that this writing was made in the reign of Amenemhet III, 1850–1800 B.C. But the date that Petrie assigns to this Pharaoh is 2432–2384 B.C. Anyhow it was at a time when intimate relations existed between Egyptians and Semites, for the Ras Shamra excavations have revealed a present this Pharaoh had made them there of a large green sphinx. Traces of this Sinai script were found on a potsherd at Gezer, and on an ostracon at Beth Shemesh by Dr. Grant. Mr. Starkey's discovery of the ewer at Tell Duweir (Lachish), illustrated in the frontispiece, with the writing also illustrated elsewhere, definitely connects the Sinai script with the Phœnician alphabet.

Professor Sprengling's pamphlet on the subject of his

THE EARLIEST ALPHABETICAL WRITING

The sphinx with this script written beneath was found at the Temple of Serabit in Sinai. The script dates back to the time of Moses, or earlier.

(Courtesy of Egypt Exploration Society.)

interpretation of the Sinai script is marred by his representing Joshua and the Israelites as destroying the evidence of writing! And the reason assigned for Moses breaking the tables of stone is a travesty of the Bible narrative!

The fact that alphabetical writing was in existence in Sinai long before Moses, and the fact that it was in use by the Semitic race to which Moses belonged, is strong presumptive evidence in favour of the Israelite use of writing in the Wilderness. So far from the Israelites having no use for writing, there are over a dozen references to the art in the books of Moses, thus:

"And the Lord said unto Moses, Write thou these words."   (Exod. xxxiv. 27.)

"Write thou every man's name on this rod."
                                                          (Num. xvii. 2.)

"Thou shalt write them upon the doorposts of thy house."   (Deut. vi. 9.)

"He shall write her a bill of divorcement."
                                                          (Deut. xxiv. 1 and 3.)

"Thou shalt write upon them (the plastered stones) all the words of this law . . . in mount Ebal."
                                                          (Deut. xxvii. 3, 4.)

"Now therefore write ye this song." (Deut. xxxi. 19.)

"And it came to pass when Moses made an end of writing the words of this law in a book."
                                                          (Deut. xxxi. 24.)

If we turn onwards to the Book of Joshua we read:

"And he (Joshua) wrote there upon the stones a copy of the law of Moses."   (Joshua viii. 32.)

Truly, Professor Sprengling should consider such passages as these before he engages in a diatribe against Moses, Joshua, and the Israelites, because "they did not learn to appreciate this glorious gift of the gods." The evidence points in the contrary direction to what he suggests to be the case.

The "glorious gift of writing" was used in the service, not only of gods, but of GOD; indeed it was used to such purpose that we can read to-day the incomparable literature of the Bible. And the account of the Fall of Jericho, as verified by the excavations, testifies to the accuracy of the writers, as well as do other accounts mentioned in this book. Is this strange complaint by Mr. Sprengling, about neglect of writing by the Israelites, a specimen of the nonsensical results obtained from the so-called Higher Criticism of the Bible?

But to return to the temple of Serabit. In his expedition of 1904–5 Sir Flinders Petrie found, from the Egyptian monuments there, that the greatest builder and patron of this temple had been the Princess Hatshepsut when associated with Thotmes III. Thus the Jericho dates have given an entirely new significance to the discovery.

In the previous chapter attention has been drawn to the probability that Moses was the favourite of Hatshepsut. Here, then, was his patroness, restoring and beautifying a temple devoted to the worship of Moses' race, in that very country to which in later years he led the Israelites. The conclusions to be drawn from these "coincidences" are, of course, conjectural, but verily, they rest on a much healthier basis than the "assured results" of the past generation of Higher Critics! They are:

(a) That Moses himself, when a young man, was well acquainted with this temple of Semitic worship in Sinai.

(b) That he used such Semitic ritual in a purified and monotheistic form for the Tabernacle in the Wilderness.

(c) That he actually used, and perhaps improved the alphabetic script.

Again, Bible students will recollect how the ten plagues of Egypt followed Moses' request to Pharaoh:

"Let us go, we pray thee, three days' journey into the desert and sacrifice unto the Lord our God."
(Exod. v. 3.)

Sir Flinders Petrie is of the opinion that "the three days' journey into the Wilderness" was the phrase used in Egypt for going down to Sinai. At a later stage in the sacred narrative we read:

"And Pharaoh called for Moses and for Aaron and said, Go ye, sacrifice to your God in the land. And Moses said, It is not meet so to do; for we shall sacrifice the abomination of the Egyptians to the Lord our God: lo, shall we sacrifice the abomination of the Egyptians before their eyes, and will they not stone us? We will go three days' journey into the Wilderness and sacrifice . . ."
(Exod. viii. 25, 27.)

Other allusions to "the abomination of the Egyptians," create the impression that the reference here is to the sacrifice of sheep. Anyhow, the passage brings out the difference between Egyptian and Israelite sacrifices.

Was Moses' pretext for taking the Israelites out of Egypt that they might sacrifice at Serabit?

As already pointed out, the evidence that the Temple of Serabit supplies of the common use of alphabetical writing among Semites at the very time of Moses, is also evidence that the great leader and lawgiver of the Israelites had means at his disposal for committing his legislation in writing to posterity, as well as the contemporary history of his race. And the writing on the Tell Duweir ewer proves that this script was brought into Palestine, and was in common use there a century and a half after Moses.

The archaic Hebrew inscriptions, written in an alphabetical language, found at Ras Shamra, employ only cuneiform, or straight wedge-shaped characters. At Serabit some of the characters are curved, and they more nearly resemble Egyptian hieroglyphics on the one hand, and the later Phœnician and Hebrew scripts on the other. If the Sinai miners were Midianites, Moses probably learned them very thoroughly during his long sojourn in that country. The script, and the system of keeping accounts, may, after all, have originally come up from Arabia.

It has been contended that the intermittent working of the Sinai mines made it unlikely that Moses ever led the Israelites into this region. But the evidence that the miners were Semites, places a different aspect upon this conjecture. It is unlikely that the mines in Sinai were being worked when the Pharaohs were spending all their time and energies in conquering Palestine and Syria. That seems to have been the course of events both before and after Israel left Egypt. But in any case, the presence of Semitic miners in Sinai was an additional guarantee for the safety of the Israelites; and that the Egyptian army would not pursue them into that inhospitable region.

The manifestations from the Unseen which accompanied the journeys of the Israelites—such as the pillar of cloud by day, and the pillar of fire by night; or the giving of the Law from Mount Sinai—are phenomena which modern writers associate with volcanic action. There is really no necessity to identify them with natural phenomena as is commonly known and recognized to-day; although even if this is done, it does not remove them from the direct action of the Deity, working through the instrumentality with which we are familiar.

But the author would identify these manifestations with phenomena as yet but imperfectly recognized, which on a far, far smaller scale are beginning to be studied at the present time. Here at that supreme moment in the history of the religion of the Israelites, there was outpoured on these people terrific evidences of the reality of that God, in whom, as St. Paul told the Athenians, we live and move, and have our being.

XV

THE EVIDENCE FROM RAS SHAMRA

THIS chapter will contain a fuller account of the important Ras Shamra inscriptions, references to which are scattered all through this volume.

In May 1929, two French archæologists, MM. Schaeffer and Chenet, in digging among the ruins of Ras Shamra in North Syria, opposite the Island of Cyprus, came across some clay tablets inscribed with a new kind of cuneiform writing. These aroused such interest, that in 1930–32, the French authorities invited these two excavators to make more extensive excavations. With a greatly augmented band of native workers, some most interesting discoveries were made among the royal tombs of the place, in the form of quantities of pottery, decorated vases, perfume bottles, carved ivory vases, toilet outfits, weapons of bronze, brooches and necklaces of gold and silver, stone altars, etc., etc. In due course the site of the city's temple was excavated; it contained a large rectangular courtyard, and a stone platform, upon which the images of gods and goddesses once stood. Remains of these were found among the ruins. Near a broad staircase pieces of a large sphinx of green stone came to light; and on

ONE OF THE RAS SHAMRA TABLETS

The writing is in alphabetical cuneiform; the language is archaic Hebrew. The date is 1400–1360 B.C., *i.e.* soon after the death of Moses.

(Courtesy of " Syria.")

its breast an inscription in Egyptian hieroglyphics to indicate that it was a gift from the Pharaoh Amenemhat III, a Pharaoh of the twelfth dynasty (Petrie's date 2432 B.C.). The association of this Pharaoh with the Temple of Serabit in Sinai, to which reference has been made in the previous chapter, also indicates that whatever his origin, he enjoyed friendly relations with the Semites whether of Phœnicia or of Sinai. And this fact is the more interesting because the Hyksos invasion of Egypt began soon after this reign.

There was also found among these ruins a portrait of a wife of another Pharaoh, about the same period, so also was a statue of a Hittite deity. In the neighbourhood of the spot where the mysterious alphabetical cuneiform tablets had been previously found, the workers ultimately came upon the contents of the temple library. The ruins of the building associated with these finds had been a school or college for scribes. Clay tablets were there, whose surfaces had obviously been used for writing exercises. Similar discoveries have been made in Babylonia; they testify to the widespread use of the art of writing in these remote ages. Others of the tablets were dictionaries or works of reference. There was also a register of ships which used the seaport. Its position opposite Cyprus, and on the mainland of Northern Syria, made Ras Shamra a cosmopolitan spot, a meeting-place of many nations. An examination of all the tablets found revealed the fact that eight languages were spoken in the city, or at any rate inscribed upon its tablets, and that the pupils at the college were taught these scripts. The languages were:

(a) The archaic Hebrew written in the cuneiform alphabetical script which forms the subject of our references.

(b) The Babylonian language in the conventional cuneiform script such as was used in the Tel el Amarna letters.

(c) The Sumerian language, which was older than the Babylonian.

(d) and (e) Two unknown languages.

(f) The Egyptian and its hieroglyphics.

(g) The Hittite, whose scripts are now being deciphered.

(h) Another unknown language which appears to hail from Cyprus and Crete.

These tablets indicate that some fifty gods, and half as many goddesses, were particularly associated with Ras Shamra. This abundance of deities recalls the bitter taunt made by Jeremiah, the prophet, many centuries later, to the Jews: "According to the number of thy cities are thy gods, O Judah!" Such is the background presented by the alphabetical cuneiform inscriptions in archaic Hebrew found at Ras Shamra. The tablets inscribed in the other seven languages only concern us in the matter of date. Mr. Theodor Gaster of London visited Paris to study these archaic Hebrew inscriptions now housed in the Louvre Museum, and the author is indebted to him for a portion of the following information. The methods employed for the decipherment of these tablets have been already described. A considerable number have not yet been published, so their full significance cannot yet be understood or appreciated. The tablets are provisionally dated between 1400–1350 B.C.; that is to say, they are thought to have been written at the same time as the Tel el Amarna tablets, and during Joshua's conquest of Canaan. The ancient name for Ras Shamra has been identified as Ugarit, a seaport which figures in various Egyptian texts, particularly in the time of Rameses II (1295–1229).

Some of these tablets contain ceremonial rituals, or liturgies, whose styles and phrasings resemble those of the Old Testament. But what is much more remarkable is the fact that the tablets refer to a number of sacrifices with which the Books of Exodus, Leviticus, Numbers, and Deuteronomy have already made us familiar. And the technical expressions, used for the sacrifices in the archaic Hebrew of these tablets, are identical with those used in the original Hebrew of the Old Testament. Here is a list:

(1) THE TRESPASS OFFERING—to which there are allusions in Leviticus v. 15; Leviticus vii. 1, 2, 5 and 37; Leviticus xiv. 12, 13: Numbers vi. 12; Numbers xviii. 19; Ezekiel xl. 39, etc.

(2) THE PEACE OFFERING. See Leviticus xxii. 21; Numbers vi. 17; Numbers xv. 8; Deuteronomy xxvii. 7.

(3) THE TRIBUTE OFFERING—to which there are allusions in Exodus xxviii. 38; Leviticus xxiii. 38 (Revised Version "gifts"); Deuteronomy xvi. 17; Ezekiel xx. 26, 31.

(4) The Wave Offering. See Exodus xxix. 24, 26; Leviticus vii. 30; Leviticus viii. 27; Leviticus ix. 21, etc.; Numbers vi. 20; Numbers viii. 15, etc.

(5) Firstfruits. See Exodus xxiii. 19; Exodus xxxiv. 26; Leviticus ii. 12; Numbers xviii. 12; Deuteronomy xxvi. 2, 10; Ezekiel xx. 40.

(6) Bread of the Gods. See Leviticus xxi. 6, 8, 17; Malachi i. 7.

(7) Burnt Offering. See Leviticus iv. 12.

(8) Whole Burnt Offerings. See Leviticus vi. 15; Deuteronomy xiii. 16–17; Deuteronomy xxxiii. 10.

(9) Offering for "Expiation of the Soul." Compare the phrasing of Leviticus iv. 2.

(10) New Moon Offering. See Numbers xxviii. 11.

In a polytheistic setting the Divine Names "El" and "Elohim" also appear often on these tablets; they are the words that occur thousands of times in the original Hebrew version of the Bible and are translated "God" in our English versions. The very first sentence in the Bible is literally: "In the beginning Elohim created the heavens and the earth."

The name "Yah" familiar to us as Jehovah, also appears in the following passage on one of the tablets: "*The name of my Son is Yah-Elat.*" . . .

The part of the tablet, on which further words of this sentence were written has been broken away; so Elat may begin another sentence and not link up with Yah; or on the other hand it may actually be Yah-Elim, in other words Jehovah-Elohim.

The tablets describe a ceremony of boiling a kid in

its mother's milk. It was intended as a milk charm; but it is expressly forbidden the Israelites—See Exodus xxiii. 19 or Deuteronomy xiv. 21.

Again there is a ritual text for offerings on the housetops to the sun, moon, and stars. The prohibition of this practice in Deuteronomy iv. 19, does not mention the housetops, since the Israelites were then dwelling in tents, but the custom is denounced later by the prophets Jeremiah and Zephaniah.

Here then are tablets written in archaic Hebrew, said to be contemporary with the time of Joshua, which contain the Divine Names, and the mention of sacrifices instituted by Moses. But the matter does not end there. References also occur to the tabernacle and furnishings similar to those which Moses provided for the Israelites in the Wilderness. The tablets refer to:

(a) THE COURTYARD OF THE TENT, which accords with the Court of the Tabernacle. See Exodus xxvii. 9; Exodus xxxv. 17; Exodus xxxviii. 9, etc.

(b) THE HOLY PLACE OF THE HOLY PLACES, which compares with the "Holy of Holies" (Exod. xxvi. 33, 34, etc.).

(c) THE TABLE OF GOLD IN THE SANCTUARY, which compares with the table overlain with gold (Exod. xxv. 24; Lev. xxiv. 6).

(d) GUESTS OF THE GODS. In the tablets the sacred enclosure was regarded as "sanctuary." The expression "Guest" is the same as used in the Bible for "stranger within the gates" (Exod. xx. 10; Deut. v. 14).

(*e*) THE PRIEST in the Ras Shamra ritual is called "Kohen," the name for the priests of the Israelites. The same word is used of Melchizedek, king of Salem, "priest of El Elyon" (Gen. xiv. 18); and of Jethro, priest of Midian (Exod. ii. 16).

(*f*) ARK OF THE COVENANT. There is an allusion in the Ras Shamra tablets to a sacred object called "Ed," round which the women worshippers danced. This may be a reference to the ark of the Covenant since the word for "Covenant" is "Eduth."

(*g*) CERTAIN OFFERINGS ON THE HEARTH OR ASHPIT which compares with Leviticus iv. 12.

(*h*) THE SACRED NUMBER SEVEN is familiar to us in connection with "the seventh day" (Exod. xx. 10), or with "the year of release" (Deut. xv. 1). It occurs frequently in the Ras Shamra tablets, where there are festivals of seven days' duration, seven years reign of the king, seven years influence of departed spirits, etc.

(*i*) THE DEAD ARE KNOWN AS "REPHAIM," a word translated both as "giants" and "dead" in the Bible. Reference to the latter usage will be found in Job xxvi. 5 or Psalm lxxxviii. 10.

(*j*) LEVIATHAN. A Ras Shamra tablet says: "Didst thou not smite Leviathan, the swift serpent, even the crooked serpent? Didst thou not break in pieces his seven heads?" The resemblance of this passage to Isaiah xxvii. 1 is exact; and an echo of it will be found in Psalm lxxiv. 14. There seem also to be allusions in Revelation xii. 3.

As if this was not enough to relate these rituals and their accessories with those of the Israelites under the leadership of Moses, some of these inscriptions refer to mystic rites and ceremonies in the wilderness of Kadesh. And it was in the same wilderness of Kadesh that the Israelites sojourned for a time in their wanderings (Num. xx. 1). According to these ancient tablets there were simultaneously born there Sahar and Salem, children of Terach the moon-god. Another tablet seems to put matters rather differently and to refer to the birth of the seventh of the great gods—Shalem Shakhar. Either way there appears to be a reference to a deity who gave his name to Jerusalem. Associated with this deity are the words "He shall upbuild Ashdod." Ashdod was near Askelon, in the south of Palestine on the Mediterranean. It is known to-day as Esdud. Once it was one of the five great Philistine cities, but the reference here is apparently to a much earlier period. The distinguished French writer— M. Dussaud—has connected the references on the tablets with a trade-route from the north end of the Gulf of Akaba on the Red Sea, through Kadesh to Ashdod—in other words, a route from the Red Sea to the Mediterranean.

Who were the people that wrote these inscriptions, and that used these sacrifices and ceremonies? On the tablets they represent themselves to be descendants of Arabs who had come from the Arabah, the district in the extreme south of Palestine around the Dead Sea which is called "the Sea of the Arabah" in Joshua

iii. 16. The following has been suggested as throwing light on this connection:

"He [King Uzziah] went forth and warred against the Philistines, and brake down the wall of Gath, and the wall of Jabneh, and the wall of Ashdod; and he built cities in the country of Ashdod, and among the Philistines. And God helped him against the Philistines, *and against the Arabians that dwelt in Gur-Baal, and the Meunim.*" (2 Chron. xxvi. 6 7.)

Uzziah was king of Judah in the days of Isaiah, a good many centuries after the dates assigned to these tablets. But the association between Ashdod and the Arabians is interesting, even though it occurs so very long after the mythological events connected with Shalem-Shasar. According to the tablet someone had destroyed Ashdod; and Shalem-Shasar was to rebuild it. It has been thought that the Philistines arrived on the coastlands of Palestine about 1200 B.C. Can there be a reference to an earlier invasion by the Cretans?

One of the Ras Shamra tablets deciphered in 1934 is known as "the Keret Tablet." It concerns Keret, king of the Sidonians, son of the god El. His father exhorts him to go forth and fight against some enemies under the command of Terah or Terach, and among them the people of the country of Zabulon are named.

Keret had no heir to succeed him, now he reluctantly consents to go and fight, when the god his father promises that he shall have a son.

Keret first offers elaborate sacrifices from the top of a tower or ziggurat, and afterwards makes provision for the town against famine, for the enemy already occupied five great fortresses. The hostile armies joined battle in the plain of Negeb, several districts are mentioned, one is called the Keretian Negeb, perhaps the Cretan Negeb. Fabulous numbers of combatants are given, including the Bedouin. The Phœnicians were defeated; entire peoples among the Canaanites were forced to migrate, in particular those in the district of Asher, to the north of Zabulon. Keret flees towards Edom. Terah or Terach sets out to occupy the land he had just conquered; but first he makes the moon rise by the command of Shin, the wife of Nekar his friend.

This is a brief résumé of M. Charles Virolleaud's interpretation of the tablet. He points out that the female Shin is the Chaldean male deity Sin. Another goddess mentioned is Nikkab, or Ningab, the wife of Sin, also venerated in Ur of the Chaldees. He also points to the analogy between Terah, the father of Abraham, who brought his people from Ur of the Chaldees into North Syria, but his successors pursuing the journey penetrated into Canaan. These facts, he writes, were not known until now, except from Genesis xi. and following, and that here we have a testimony to the truth of the Sacred Narrative. So that in future it will not be allowable to write that the Jews caused Abraham to come out of Chaldea, famous for arts and sciences, in order to give their ancestor such an honour.

Such is briefly what has been said of the Keret tablet. Any further endeavour to get behind this mythology is, of course, highly speculative. Reference has already been made to the fact that the name of the god Shalem, used in another mythological tablet, dates it back before Abraham. Sinai is a name that has always been associated with Sin the moon-god. The Negeb was in South Palestine. The following is a conjecture of what may have happened: If as early Rabbinical tradition suggests, Terah or Terach was a great military leader, he would be a leader of Habiru mercenaries, perhaps Hyksos. So the story may combine an echo of his victory, as well as the far more recent invasion of Canaan under Joshua in which the tribes of Zebulon and Asher participated. The territory in which these two tribes were settled by Joshua is the territory referred to in the poem. There is the passage in the blessing of Jacob:

"Zebulon shall dwell at the beach of the sea and his border shall be upon Zidon." (Gen. xlix. 13.)

There is an ancient tradition which represented the Phœnicians as being descended from sojourners round the neighbourhood of the Dead Sea, who fled to the Syrian coast in consequence of the cataclysm that destroyed Sodom and Gomorrah. In the chapter on Abraham it will be seen that this disaster occurred about 2061 B.C.

That seems to accord with the history of these Arabs from the Arabah. But Ras Shamra was such a polyglot place that there may be confusion in anything so definite. Again, have we to do here with Midianites, those people among whom Moses lived for forty years, and to whom considerable reference has been made in a previous chapter?

From the information at our disposal, it would seem that the authors of these pagan ritual, ceremonial, and other tablets, may have imitated quite a good deal of the ritual and sacrifices instituted by Moses; and copied as well still earlier rituals such as used by Abraham, by Melchizedek, king of Salem, and probably also by Jethro, the priest of Midian.

The earliest date assigned to these tablets is from forty to eighty years after the promulgation of the Law on Mount Sinai. What happened to Moses and to the Israelites in the Wilderness must have become known to those associated with his religion and race elsewhere. The account of these tremendous manifestations in Sinai would be noised abroad, first to the neighbouring country of Midian, and then conveyed by Midianite merchants to their kinsmen in Phœnicia.

These "Arabs," at this important seaport of Ras Shamra, would hear about the phenomena associated with Moses, and be eager to reproduce his rituals and ceremonies. With fifty-five gods, and twenty-five goddesses of their own, and eight different languages, this ancient college of writing that MM. Schaeffer and Chenet unearthed, seems to have been nothing more nor less than a theological seminary. The fact that information did come from Sinai to Ras Shamra soon after Moses is supplied by the alphabetical script. It is evident that the people of Ras Shamra had heard rumours about the Sinai alphabet, and attempted to reproduce it in the cuneiform characters to which they were accustomed.

Nevertheless the Bible itself supplies evidence of the earlier Semitic ritual in existence long before Moses. And what applies to ritual, archæology has proved, applies also to the laws instituted by Moses. Thus the code of Hammurabi, promulgated in the days of Abraham, bears resemblances to the Mosaic code of laws. Hammurabi's code of laws, engraved upon a diorite stele eight feet high, illustrated elsewhere, was discovered some thirty years ago at Susa, whither the Elamites had carried it for plunder.

The further excavations made by Dr. Schaeffer during the year 1933 have brought to light two splendid gold vases which are dated between 1400–1200 B.C., and which are engraved with mythological and animal characters. He has also definitely identified the city with the ancient seaport of Ugarit. More tablets have been found. One of them deals with the diseases of horses. One remedy prescribed is a poultice made from figs called "debelet." It is suggested that this is the remedy prescribed by the prophet Isaiah for King Hezekiah in the following passage:

"And Isaiah said, Take a cake of figs. And they took and laid it on the boil, and he [Hezekiah] recovered."
(2 Kings xx. 7.)

A section has now been dug into the Ras Shamra mound from the top to virgin soil. This enabled a study to be made of the different strata, representing the ruins of different cities superimposed one above the other. The upper levels belong to the period of Egypt's eighteenth and nineteenth dynasties (1573 to 1200 B.C.), the next belong to the time of the Hyksos or Shepherd Kings, and the lower to the twelfth dynasty of Egypt (2584–2371 B.C. [Petrie]).

To conclude this chapter; it is obvious that the critical conclusions, concerning the late date of the Mosaic ritual, and the tabernacle worship, look ridiculous in the light of this discovery.

In some of the tablets parallels are discernible with contemporary Israelite history. Thus:

(a) The Israelites enter Canaan after staying in Kadesh, where these Arabs claim to have once held their rites.

(b) The conflict between the Sidonians and Terah is recalled, when Zebulon and Asher, the descendants of Terah, have just settled near Sidon.

(c) The ritual and ceremonial are imitations of those instituted by Moses.

XVI

EVIDENCES OF RELIGION BEFORE MOSES

IT has already been suggested that the Bible makes much contact with a region which has been far less explored than Palestine—let us call it the land of the Unseen. The radio is beginning to make us familiar with its reality; at any rate, to make us understand that what is invisible to our eye has nevertheless both potentialities and possibilities.

But mankind has always been in contact with the Unseen through some of his senses. The unsound materialistic teaching of the past generation obscured this great fact of existence. Too much emphasis was placed on what was dubbed "Reason," and too little on Intuition. Yet Feelings and Emotions always play a greater part in our lives than we care to recognize. One who has been engaged in industry and commerce from his youth up has noticed the conspicuous part that sentiment plays in business, despite many assertions to the contrary.

Associated with the emotions are the senses of Beauty, in Nature as well as in Art. Such senses connect us with Poetry, Literature, Music, Painting, Sculpture, Drama, etc. Some people lack one or more of these senses, even as there are those who are colour blind.

Writing of colour will remind us that colours come from the light; and that what to us represent colours, are merely mediums which select and reflect the coloured rays from the light prism. It is significant to find that nearly all the great masters of the Arts have claimed that they were more in the nature of mediums for the transmission of something that reached them from the Unseen, rather than the actual originators of their work. To put this idea into radio language— the great poets, writers, musicians, painters, sculptors, actors, etc., appear to have inside them receiving stations that can tune in to various types of vibrations which we call "Celestial Ray" wave-lengths. These communications the artist in turn transmits to his fellow-creatures, and to posterity. Even so do Nature's flowers each reflect its own particular colours from the light. Here again, let us pause to observe that just as there are those who are colour blind, so there are also those who have no sense of poetry; or no sense of music; and so on.

Now besides receptivity to these art vibrations, if they may be so called, there exists receptivity to other types of communications. The author is, of course, aware that those who have had no experience, nor taken the trouble to study such matters, represent these other types as all fraudulent. So would our grand-parents have dubbed the electrical results which we obtain to-day from the radio. But these other types have been well attested, both in history and in present-day experiences, by the Psychical Research Society and other organizations. They consist of words from the Unseen, visions from the Unseen, writing received other than through one's ordinary intelligence, and the gift of foretelling events. Associated with receptivity to this class of phenomena, as it is also with the art senses, are the religious senses, which are widespread, at any rate, in the young. What we call Conscience plays a leading part in such religious manifestations, as well as Faith, Hope, Love, Joy and Peace, etc.—gifts which religious-minded people rightly associate with the Holy Spirit.

But here let us notice that contact with the Unseen *does not always imply contact with Truth.*

Take, for example, the dramatic passage in the Bible where King Ahab asks Micaiah:—

" Shall we go up to Ramoth-gilead to battle?"

The prophet prefaces his reply with the words:—

"I saw the Lord sitting on his throne, and all the host of heaven standing by him on the right hand and on the left . . . and there came forth a spirit and . . . said . . . I will go forth and will be a lying spirit in the mouth of all his [Ahab's] prophets."

(1 Kings xxii. 19 to 22.)

Or for those who prefer the New Testament, there is the passage that foreshadows the culmination of the ages:

"And there was war in heaven: Michael and his angels fought against the dragon; and the dragon warred, and his angels." (Rev. xii. 7.)

Many other passages might be quoted to indicate that the Unseen includes Evil as well as Good.

It is desirable also to emphasize that all religions seem to involve contact with the Unseen. Many people are under the impression that there is nothing behind all the ceremonies and superstitions of other religions. That is incorrect. There is contact made with all sections of the Unseen, from the highest to the lowest. This constitutes the danger of what is to-day known as Spiritualism. In reading the life of Mahomet, written by men who have no knowledge of Spiritualism, it is quite obvious that Mahomet was what Spiritualists call a Medium; he made contact with the Unseen; and evolved from it a religion which is believed to-day by a vast portion of the human race; and which contains many good points. Another man who made contact with the Unseen, in a similar way, was Balaam, who was fetched to curse the Israelites in the Wilderness, and blessed them. Yet another was David, who actually writes:

"All this have I been made to understand in writing from the hand of Jehovah."
(1 Chron. xxviii. 19; Rev. Vers.)

Put in plain modern language, David exercised a gift well known to psychical research—the gift of automatic writing.

The gift of prophecy, or of foretelling, or of second sight, which is ignored by Bible critics, is also a well-known feature of contact with the Unseen. Instances abound throughout history—pagan as well as Christian. To-day people call such happenings "coincidences." How many coincidences are required to lift such phenomena out of the region of chance into one more interesting? Those who smile at such things are unaware of the trend of modern science.

To return to archæology: as a result of his study of cuneiform tablets, Dr. Langdon writes:

"In Sumerian and Semitic religions, monotheism preceded polytheism and belief in good and evil spirits." (*Semitic Religion*, xviii.)

So in the study of religion, as presented to us in the ancient cuneiform writings before the time of Moses, a great mixture of good and evil, of rites and ceremonies going back to primeval times, must be expected. Some of these had been debased, and distorted, and lost their original significance, through the intervention of influences from the Unseen which were not wholly good, and in some cases, were very evil. Great emphasis is laid upon this matter by Moses speaking to the Israelites in the Wilderness:

"When thou are come into the land which the Lord thy God giveth thee, thou shalt not learn to do after the abominations of those nations. There shall not be found among you anyone that maketh his son or his daughter to pass through the fire, one that useth divination, or an observer of times, or an enchanter, or a witch, or a charmer, or a consulter with familiar spirits, or a wizard, or a necromancer. . . . For these nations which thou shalt possess, hearkened unto observers of times, and unto diviners; but as for thee, the Lord thy God hath not suffered thee so to do."

(Deut. xviii. 9–14.)

It is probably on account of the condemnation contained in such passages as these, that there are comparatively few references to primitive Semitic religion before the days of Moses in the Old Testament. At the same time, there are enough to indicate that the religion of Moses contained a revival of former Semitic ritual and ceremonies, cleansed and purified for the use of the Israelites. The most primitive religious ceremonies recorded in the Bible are the sacrifices of Cain and Abel (Gen. iv.). It would seem as though after Adam had been cast out of Paradise, some sense of propitiation was felt to be necessary. In Cain it took the form of the sacrifice of the fruit of the ground; in Abel the first of his sheep. Here then is the institution of sacrifices—of First Fruits, and of the Sin and Peace Offerings, in the most remote period of the human race. After the Flood it is stated:

"And Noah builded an altar unto the Lord; and took of every clean beast, and every clean fowl, and offered burnt offerings on the altar." (Gen. viii. 20.)

It is therefore quite obvious that all kinds of sacrifices formed part of the primeval and primitive religion of mankind.

And let us remind ourselves of the further fact that before the days of Noah there are records of an intimate contact with the Unseen, not in these cases with mixed influences of Good and Evil, but with the Holiest and Highest. Thus it is written:

"And Enoch walked with God after he begat Methuselah, three hundred years, and begat sons and daughters; . . . and Enoch walked with God: and he was not; for God took him." (Gen. v. 22, 24.)

Observe that the expression "walked with God" is twice repeated, as though to emphasize a close and intimate communion with the Unseen over three hundred years. The writer of the Epistle to the Hebrews summarizes these happenings in thrilling strains of triumph:

"By faith Abel offered unto God a more excellent sacrifice than Cain . . . and he being dead yet speaketh. By faith Enoch was translated that he should not see death . . . for he hath had witness borne to him that before his translation he had been well pleasing unto God." (Heb. xi. 4, 5.)

And so the honour roll of Faith ran from Abel and Enoch, through Noah and Abraham, on to Moses. Those who assume that the Hebrew religion began with Moses, overlook these Bible proofs of an earlier religion; of earlier sacred ceremonies and sacrifices; and earlier intercourse with the Divine. "Enoch walked with God!" What possibilities of divine revelation are implied during the three hundred years in which Enoch enjoyed this association.

In consequence of that unfortunate theory of the evolution of religion, modern writers have failed to realize how those days before and after the Flood were not all evil days. There was a Golden Age, to which the ancient classical writers make references. Now archæological evidence of such times, from the older Egyptian monuments, is being brought to our notice. The walls of the galleries and rooms in the interior of the pyramids of Sakkara are covered with hieroglyphic writings, which are dated back to the period 3500–2500 B.C., and perhaps earlier. These writings testify to a very high standard of religion. They display a conception of Righteousness and Justice such as we are familiar with in the Book of Deuteronomy, the Book of Job, the Psalms, the Proverbs, Isaiah, etc. Did Moses read these writings? It is quite probable. But Bible readers can trace them back to an earlier source. They are relics of the Golden Age; of the outpourings from the Unseen; of the days when Enoch walked with God. What evidence they give of a belief in a future life! How they certify to the presence and influence of intelligences altogether beyond those of the Egyptian fellahin!

So it is not surprising that the Ras Shamra inscriptions contain a strange jumble of the Bible sacrifices and ceremonies, mingled with the gross beliefs in pagan gods and goddesses. It is what a study of the Bible has led us to expect. It confirms Dr. Langdon's conclusions about Good and Evil Spirits derived from a study of the Babylonian tablets. It confirms too the teaching of Anthropology as set down in Dr. Schmidt's book, *The Origin and Growth of Religion*.

In the Epistle to the Hebrews we are reminded that

Abraham paid tithes to Melchizedek, king of Salem
(Heb. vii. 4). That would be six centuries before
Moses instituted them. Dr. Barton of Philadelphia has
recently suggested that the ritual "Bread and Wine"
ceremony, set down on one of the Ras Shamra tablets,
may have actually been used by Melchizedek when he
met Abraham.

Many years ago H. Clay Trumbull, of Philadelphia,
pointed out that the Passover was a most ancient rite,
which can be traced back to what is still, to us, the
twilight period of religion. And when the sacred text
is carefully examined, it is seen to presume the previous
existence of some such ceremony.

The Ten Commandments themselves contain traces
of the past, thus :

" Thou shalt have no other gods before me."
(Exod. xx. 3.)

The need for the injunction is apparent in the light
cast by Ras Shamra excavations upon the surroundings
of these people who spoke archaic Hebrew like the
Israelites. Or, again, there is the evidence of idolatry,
and Baal worship, among the Semitic miners at the
very time of Moses, in that same Sinai, at the Temple
of Serabit. The like observation applies to the Commandment :

" Thou shalt not make unto thee a graven
image." (verse 4.)

It was not alone the graven images of the Egyptians,
but those of their own race, against which Israel was

THE PEAK OF JEBAL MUSA IN THE PENINSULA OF SINAI

Which tradition claims to be the mountain of Sinai from which the Ten Commandments were spoken.

warned. The Fourth Commandment is even more impressive.

" Remember the sabbath day to keep it holy."
(verse 8.)

The very word "remember" presupposes that the Sabbath Day was already in existence, as we know to have been the case in Babylonia:

"In the official calendars the seventh, fourteenth, twenty-first, and twenty-eighth days, have special rubrics." (Langdon's *Semitic Mythology*, p. 153.)

And allusion has already been made to the sacredness of the number seven at Ras Shamra.

The incident of these Ten Commandments spoken in a tremendous voice from Mount Sinai, is a unique example of Manifestation from the Unseen. In the light of present-day knowledge the phenomena have ceased to be incredible. The words spoken carry their own evidence of the source from which they were derived. But even they may have been a reiteration of earlier moral laws to regulate the relations between God and man, and between man and man; stern it is true, but essential for the welfare and happiness of the human race. Christ breathed into them a Spirit of Love, already foreshadowed in such passages as:

"The Lord did not set his love upon you, nor choose you because ye were more in number than any people; for ye were the fewest of all peoples: *but because the Lord loveth you.*" (Deut. vii. 7, 8.)

And it is necessary to remind many of our preachers to-day that these expressions of Love are not confined to the New Testament alone. They ring also through the Old Testament. Thus even Jeremiah the prophet, lamenting over the sins of Israel, writes:

"The Lord hath appeared of old unto me saying: '*Yea, I have loved thee with an everlasting love*: therefore with loving-kindness have I drawn thee.'" (Jer. xxxi. 3.)

Or again:

"When Israel was a child then I loved him, and called my son out of Egypt. . . . *How shall I give thee up, Ephraim? How shall I deliver thee, Israel?*"
(Hos. xi., 1 and 8.)

And so one might continue. It has been one of the bitter fruits of the so-called Higher Criticism, that such messages of Love in the Old Testament have been suppressed. But to return to the Ten Commandments, Christ so far from superseding them declared:

"Think not that I came to destroy the law or the prophets: I came not to destroy but to fulfil. For verily I say unto you, Till heaven and earth pass away, one jot or one tittle shall in no wise pass away from the Law, till all things be accomplished." (Matt. v. 17, 18.)

Such is the verification of Jesus Christ for the reality of the contents of the Old Testament.

A difficulty may arise in the minds of our readers regarding the repeated statements in the Books of Exodus, Leviticus, Numbers, and Deuteronomy that "The Lord said unto Moses." We know to-day that many of the rites and ceremonies, and indeed legislation, enacted under this authority were, at least to some extent, already in existence. The obvious suggestion is that Moses himself was responsible for their adaptation to future Israelite worship and legislation. This difficulty is due to the fact that people, either do not know, or else overlook, the fact of communications from the Unseen, to which reference has been made in the earlier part of this chapter, and elsewhere in this book.

It has already been pointed out that David claimed to have received the dimensions of Solomon's temple, through what is known to-day as "automatic writing." This gift of writing has been well authenticated by the Science of Psychical Research. The nature of "Inspiration," to which reference has also been made, was long ago discussed in the *Hibbert Journal*. In this connection Bible students might consider the question of how all the prophetic books of the Old Testament were written. Moses was the instrument appointed to carry out this great revival of Monotheism among the Israelite branch of the Semitic race. He received instructions from the Unseen, perhaps like David by automatic writing, perhaps as the Prophets received them. Those instructions contained the modification and adaptation of already existing Semitic rituals, ceremonies, and legislation, for the worship and the service of God Host High.

It will be remembered that Moses' first communication from the Unseen occurred when he saw the Burning

Bush at the back of Mount Horeb. At that time in answer to Moses' inquiry:

"When I come unto the children of Israel, and shall say unto them, The God of your fathers hath sent me unto you; and they shall say to me, what is His name? What shall I say unto them? And God said unto Moses I AM WHO AM. . . . And God said moreover, Jehovah the God of your fathers has sent me unto you."   (Exod. iii. 13–15, margin R.V.)

At a later date the following was given:

"And God spake unto Moses and said unto him — I am Jehovah; and I appeared unto Abraham, unto Isaac, and unto Jacob, as God Almighty [Hebrew *El Shaddai*], but by my name Jehovah I was not known unto them."
                                    (Exod. vi. 2.)

Long before Abraham, of the days of Enos the grandson of Adam, it is written:

"Then began men to call upon the name of Jehovah."
                                    (Gen. iv. 26.)

It may be presumed that this name for the Deity fell into disuse before the Patriarchal period. Langdon tells us that the word Jehovah is incorrect. He writes:

"In the sacred writings of the Jews this original name is correctly preserved in proper names as Yaw and Yah, but for some unexplained reason it was extended into a verbal form, apparently Yahweh, 'He causes to be,' and then pointed with the vowels of the word 'Adonai,' and pronounced Adōnai, whence the modern reading Jehovah." (*Semitic Mythology*, p. 43.)

This remarkable conclusion of the Professor of Assyriology at Oxford, made several years ago, has just been verified by those Ras Shamra tablets to which such frequent reference is made in these pages. Attention has already been drawn to the fact that the Divine Name "Yah," occurs in these fourteenth-century B.C. documents. Another instance occurs in a cuneiform letter from Taanach (a place mentioned in Deborah's Song over Sisera's defeat—see Judges v. 19) of about 1500 B.C. in the proper name Ahiyami.

So the Divine Name translated Lord, or Jehovah is, after all, "Yah," or "Jah," and we are reminded of a passage in the Psalms:

"Praise him in his name Jah and rejoice before him." (Ps. lxviii. 4; Prayer Book Version.)

It has been suggested that in the name of Yah we have the original deity Ea, for Ea was the god of all mystic learning, and the Mummo, or creative word—Logos—referred to in the opening of John's Gospel: "In the beginning was the Word (*Logos*)." Thus, like the Bread of Life and Water of Life, the New Testament message is linked to the twilight "before Abraham was."

But to return to Moses—enough evidence has now been laid bare through archæology to satisfy any open-minded person that the only anachronism

involved in the Pentateuch records, is Moses' intercourse
with the Unseen. But the Unseen constantly obtrudes
in the narratives in the New Testament; is there
anything more remarkable in the incident of the
Burning Bush, than in, for example, the conversion of
St. Paul (Acts ix)? Are we, therefore, to reject both
New and Old Testaments, in deference to a legacy of
materialistic conceptions of the universe, now abandoned
by Science?

XVII

THE EVIDENCE FROM TEL EL AMARNA

SUCH are the evidences, and such the explanations that concern Moses—the great Lawgiver. Let us return to the career of his successor—Joshua—and consider further evidence connected with his conquest of Canaan. The temple of Serabit in the Peninsula of Sinai, though discovered long ago, has gained significance through the Jericho chronology. In like manner so do the Tel el Amarna letters, which were found in Egypt. Several allusions have already been made in these pages to these documents, and they require, and deserve, more notice.

The place—Tel el Amarna was once the new metropolis of Egypt, built by Amenhetep IV, better known as Akhenaton, to supersede the royal city of Thebes. It is a matter of general knowledge that this Pharaoh revived a primitive and much purer form of Religion. The worship of numerous deities, and their idols, was superseded by the worship of the Aten or solar disc. How far this cult came from Syria, and how far it was a revival of primitive belief, need not be discussed here. But the Reformation was accompanied by a wonderful revolution in the artistic life of Egypt. It is to be regretted that it all went to pieces after Akhenaton's

death; Tel el Amarna was abandoned by his successor
—Tutankhamen—and this mushroom city was deserted.

It was amid these remains of Tel el Amarna, in the
year 1888, an old peasant woman came across the
ruins of what had once been Akhenaton's Record Office.
She found there a group of three hundred and twenty
clay tablets, inscribed with cuneiform writing, and in
the Babylonian language. Of these, eighty-two are
now in the British Museum, one hundred and sixty
in Berlin, sixty in the Gizeh Museum and the rest in
private hands. During the last few years, further
excavation on the site of Tel el Amarna has been
carried on by Mr. Pendlebury for the Egypt Exploration
Society, in co-operation with the Brooklyn Museum of
Fine Arts. In the winter of 1933–4, still more excavation was made of this Record Office, built of
stamped bricks, which leave no doubt that it was "the
house of the king's correspondence." As a consequence,
nine more fragments of cuneiform correspondence were
discovered. While later on, and elsewhere, a further
piece was found.

Another building at Tel el Amarna has been identified
as having been the University. The ruins of palaces,
temples, mansions, and hotels, had already been discovered, and now the remains of the royal stables have
also been found. This affords some idea of recent work
at Tel el Amarna, as described in the *Journal of Egyptian
Archæology* to which the author is indebted. The tablets
found in 1888 are those referred to in these pages as
the Tel el Amarna tablets: and they proved on

AERIAL PHOTOGRAPH OF THE RUINS OF TEL EL AMARNA, IN EGYPT

Where the Tel el Amarna letters, written to the Pharaohs asking for help against Joshua's invasion, were found.

(Royal Air Force official—Crown copyright reserved.)

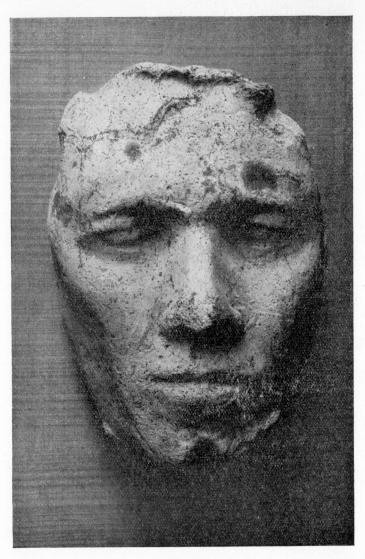

AMENHETEP III
(1413–1377 B.C.)

He ruled in Egypt when Joshua captured Jericho, and some of the Tel el Amarna
letters from the kings of Canaan appealing for help against the invading Habiru,
or Israelites, were addressed to him.

(Courtesy of State Museum, Berlin.)

decipherment to consist of letters from the kings and governors of Palestine and Syria addressed to both Amenhetep III and Amenhetep IV (Akhenaton).

It has already been stated that after the death of Princess Hatshepsut, Thotmes III turned his attention to the conquest of Palestine and Syria. Again and again, he invaded these countries; again and again he defeated their inhabitants in battle and captured their walled cities. His successors, Amenhetep II (the Pharaoh of the Exodus) and Thotmes IV, consolidated the results obtained from his conquests. Thus, both Palestine and Syria had come under the dominion of Egypt, and their petty kings had become vassals of the reigning Pharaoh.

The letters found at Tel el Amarna, addressed to the next Pharaohs—Amenhetep III and IV (Akhenaton)— abound in appeals from these petty kings, and local rulers, to their suzerain lord the Pharaoh, for help against invaders. Here is a specimen from Abdkiba, king of Jerusalem:

"As long as ships were upon the sea the strong arm of the king occupied Nahrima and Kas, but now the Habiru are occupying the king's cities. There remains not one prince to my lord the king, everyone is ruined. Behold Turbasa has been slain at the gate of Zilu and the king remains inactive! Behold Zimrida of Lachish —his servants are seeking to seize him in order to kill him" (Tablet 181).

The letters from Syria imply that the invaders were in league with the Hittites from the north. The rulers

of the many Phœnician and other cities of Syria, seem
to have engaged in intrigue with them, and with each
other, and between times to have appealed to Egypt
for help. The records indicate much duplicity. The
growing power of the Hittites will be noticed in the
next chapter. But of more concern to us are the tablets
like the one quoted above, which refer to the simultaneous invasion from Transjordania of those people
called the Habiru. For many years it has been suggested that those invaders were the Hebrews under
Joshua, the evidence that Jericho fell about 1400 B.C. in
the middle of the reign of one of the Pharaohs to whom
these letters were addressed, now definitely establishes
that identification. The conclusion that the Habiru were
the Hebrews, had already been reached by Dr. Langdon
on independent grounds. His crucial statement has
already been quoted, but is worth repeating here:

"The Hebrew deity El . . . whose name occurs
quite regularly in the plural Elohim . . . is the god
of the Habiru, a people who appear in various kingdoms
and local city dynasties of Babylonia and Assyria from
2200 B.C. . . . I am entering on debatable ground
here when I assume that the Hebrews and their god
Illani (plural always written ideographically) are
identical with the Habiru and their God Elohim.
There seems no doubt at all that this was the case. . . .
Accepting this thesis, the Hebrews had served for six
centuries as mercenary soldiers and traders among the
Babylonians, Assyrians, etc. . . . *before they entered and
occupied Canaan*" [1] (*Semitic Mythology*, p. 72).

[1] These italics are not in the original; they are merely inserted to
emphasize the part of the statement that applies to Joshua's invasion.

232

So this quotation also applies to these Tel el Amarna letters, in further confirmation of the identification of the Habiru with the Hebrews, or Israelites, under Joshua. For there is no mistake about it, the Israelites were Hebrews, not traders such as the Phœnicians, nor soldiers like the Hyksos, but devoted to more pastoral pursuits; and only now emerging from the desert, and only assuming the garb of war for the invasion of their Promised Land. The Habiru also appear to have come from the direction of Mount Seir, the same route as that traversed by the Israelites. It is difficult, and indeed impossible, because the dates are so identical, any longer to resist the conclusion that so far as Canaan is concerned, the Tel el Amarna letters contain Canaanite, Amorite, and Jebusite accounts of the Israelite invasion—versions of the Bible story written by the other side.

The accounts are hard to decipher and fit together. The German scholar, J. A. Knudtzon, in 1915, published the most complete translation, but these tablets need to be deciphered and rearranged in the light of the Jericho discoveries. Their turns of phrase often remind us of expressions in the Pentateuch, and they do contain some names that occur in the Book of Joshua. An article recently appeared in a well-known agnostic English journal which said in effect: Find the name of David or Solomon or Joshua among these contemporary inscriptions and we will believe! Here, then, in these Tel el Amarna letters, is the name of Joshua.

It would appear that the writer of the letter is one Mut Baal, who seems to have been a chieftain of the Jordan valley. The letter was addressed to Ianhamu, an Egyptian governor of Palestine. Mut Baal had informed the Egyptian that Aiah, the king of Pella, had fled before him. Pella was once an important stronghold on the east side of the Jordan valley not so far below the Lake of Galilee; reference has already been made to some trial excavations there, in which the author has been interested. But to continue our story, Ianhamu doubted the correctness of the news. Mut Baal replies:

"As the king my lord liveth, as the king my lord liveth, Aiah is not in Pella. For two months he has been in hiding. Ask then Benenima, ask then Tadua, ask then Jashuia."

Aiah is Job, Benenima is Benjamin, and Jashuia is Joshua. How to interpret the allusion is another matter. It seems to suggest that at the time, the Pharaoh's endeavours to pacify the country made Egyptian influence friendly towards Joshua. On the other hand, Mut Baal may have intended to convey the impression that, since the Egyptian governor was not taking effective steps to combat the Israelite invasion, he was obviously in alliance with them! Certainly the glimpses one gains from these Tel el Amarna tablets, of the pack of rascals that had been governing Palestine and Syria for Egypt, suggest that the ruling Pharaoh would not be sorry to see them replaced by a God-fearing people like the Israelites.

This line of thought leads us to refer to the Egyptian history of the period.

It has already been stated that the two Pharaohs to whom these letters were addressed were Amenhetep III (1413–1377 B.C.) and Amenhetep IV, better known as Akhenaton (1377–1361 B.C.). They were both connected by marriage with Syria and further north. The wife of Amenhetep III was Queen Tiy. She was the daughter of Yua and Tuau, two celebrated characters in Egyptian history. Their origin is obscure to us. The late Arthur Weigall, who was Chief Inspector of Antiquities in Egypt, in his book, *Akhnaton, Pharaoh of Egypt*, to which the author is indebted for the following, wrote that Yua was probably a Syrian prince whom the conqueror Thotmes III brought to Egypt and educated. The name is not Egyptian, and may have been Yaa or Yau. He became priest of Min, a deity which in his form Min-Ra, was a god of the sun. In this respect he resembled the Greek Adonis. Yua's wife, Tuau, may have had Egyptian royal blood in her veins, and been a granddaughter of Thotmes III.

Yua's mummy has been found and photographed, and the reproduction at any rate shows him a person of commanding personality. Queen Tiy received honours which were not even accorded to queens of the royal blood, and her descent must have been a high one. In the early years of Akhenaton, this queen was practically supreme.

The wife of Amenhetep IV (Akhenaton) was a daughter of Dushratta, king of Mitanni. Her name was Tadukhiba, renamed Nefertiti in Egypt. The rulers of Mitanni belonged to an Indro-European group of nations, who worshipped Indra, Mitra (Mithra), and Varuna, familiar in these times as the Indian trinity.

Whatever may have been the influence from 1400 B.C. onwards, the Egyptian court was being transformed by a religious revival, closely akin to Monotheism, by a new and wonderful art, and by a cosmopolitan element. The virile nationalism needed to drive out the Hyksos, and to pursue them into Palestine and Syria, and to conquer and control those countries, had for the time being exhausted itself. It was succeeded by a more enlightened outlook on religion, and on life. When Amenhetep II, after the death of the mighty Thotmes III, the oppressor of Israel, refused to let Israel go, he was surrounded by very different influences to those grouped around Amenhetep III forty years later, when Israel began to enter Canaan. As time went on, and the new religion spread, the influences already at work in the Egyptian court would grow stronger, and the hostility of the polytheistic Egyptian priests would tend to discredit similar faiths as practised in Palestine and Syria—at Ras Shamra, for example. On the other hand, Amenhetep III must have known that Moses and the Israelites in the Wilderness had adopted an even stricter form of Monotheism than he was taking up. And the first thirteen years of this Pharaoh's reign corresponded with the last thirteen years of the life of Moses. Startling as it

AMENHETEP IV (AKHENATON)
(1377–1361 B.C.)

He ruled Egypt when the remainder of the Tel el Amarna letters were written by the kings of Canaan, appealing for help against the invading Habiru, or Israelites.

(Courtesy of State Museum, Berlin.)

may sound at first to Bible students, there were good religious reasons for at least a benevolent neutrality, between the Egyptians and Israelites, during the momentous years while the latter were conquering the grossly polytheistic Canaanites and Amorites.

The age of Amenhetep IV became an age of Poetry as well as Art. And the best poem extant of the period is known as Akhenaton's Hymn. Passages of it so resemble, and so run parallel with, Psalm 104 in the Bible, that there seems no doubt they are both derived from a common Syrian source.

So there may well have been powerful considerations favourable to the Israelites, influencing Amenhetep III and his son. But one naturally wonders why no reference is made to them in the Bible. This enigma of Egyptian relationship with the Israelites, forty years after the Exodus, when Egyptian memories of that humiliation had been replaced by subsequent triumphs elsewhere, culminating in the first thirteen glorious years of Amenhetep III, will be discussed further in the next chapter. Reasons will be suggested for the conspicuous silence of the Sacred Narrative in regard to Egyptian influence on the Israelites' fortunes in Palestine.

XVIII

THE ENIGMA OF JUDGES

IT has been seen that so far the archæological evidence found tends to confirm the Old Testament narrative of the lives of Moses and Joshua; and if Egyptian history is invoked, even to illumine it.

It has now become necessary to ascertain to what extent the chronology elucidated suits later events. How far can the Book of Judges be reconciled with Egyptian history?

After the reigns of Amenhetep III and Amenhetep IV (Akhenaton), and the incidents referred to in the Tel el Amarna letters, so far as Palestine affairs are concerned, the remaining Pharaohs of the eighteenth dynasty can be passed over, all except Tutankhamen (1351–1339 B.C.). His reign began after the death of Joshua, and with the assistance of his general Horemheb, he seems to have had some success in Palestine.

It will be remembered that this Pharaoh's tomb was discovered intact some years ago by Lord Carnarvon and Mr. Howard Carter; and the marvellous gold ornaments and jewellery which it contained enable us to form some conception of the magnificence of the Egyptian court of those days. Those who have not had the good fortune to see these splendid finds in the

Cairo Museum, will yet have read of them, and seen their photographs. They enable us to form a real impression of the surroundings in which Moses must have lived a century and a half earlier.

There were two finds in this tomb of Tutankhamen which deserve a passing notice. The first was the presence of writing brushes and writing materials for the use of the deceased in the next world. The second was some small pieces of iron. It is true that Tutankhamen reigned about fifty years after the death of Moses; but those who have doubted the existence of writing of this character, and the knowledge of iron at this period, are confronted with this evidence.

A good deal is heard about the Hittites in the Old Testament. In 1906 their royal library was discovered at their capital, Boghaz Keui, in Asia Minor, about one hundred and fifty miles south of the Black Sea. Its tablets were written in the cuneiform script in eight different languages. Among them is believed to be a letter from Tutankhamen's widow, inviting the king of the Hittites to send one of his sons for her to marry now that her husband was dead. Egyptian history records the fact that Tutankhamen contested the supremacy over Syria with the Hittites, who had become a very formidable rival in the north of Asia Minor. But the remainder of the eighteenth dynasty of Egypt let Palestine and Syria alone, and so did not interfere with the affairs of the Israelites.

It is the records left of Egyptian intervention in Palestine by the nineteenth dynasty, which create the problems. In order to give a proper setting to the picture, the names and dates of its Pharaohs are here set down according to Sir Flinders Petrie's latest chronology:

NINETEENTH DYNASTY

Rameses I	1318–1317
Seti I	1317–1295
Rameses II	1295–1229
Mernepthah	1229–1210
Seti II	1210–1205
Amenmessu	1205–1204
Tausert	1204–1197

The first of these Pharaohs is recorded as building a temple at Bethshean. Our Bibles tell us that:

"Manasseh did not drive out the inhabitants of Bethshean." (Judges i. 27.)

But when reference is made to Bethshean on the map of Palestine, it will be seen that it is situated quite a good way up to the north. How did the Egyptians come to be there? An Egyptian settlement in the Promised Land, after the Israelites were settled there, seems strange. And matters get worse in the reign of the next king, Seti I, who made quite an expedition into Palestine, and besides occupying Bethshean, took Yenoam and Hamath respectively, north and south of it, as well as Acre on the sea coast. One could have understood all these happenings in the time of Thotmes III; but now that Israel has entered and occupied the Promised Land it is incredible. And not one single word about it in the Book of Judges!

The record of Egyptian presence in the north of Palestine continues and increases during the reign of Rameses II; and farther north those who visit Syria can still see this Pharaoh's inscription at the Dog River, a few miles above Beirut. Again, Bethshean was occupied, and refortified, and adorned with temples and monuments.

Rameses II's very long reign of sixty-five years was followed by that of Mernepthah, whose stele in the British Museum records that:

"The Hittite Land is at peace—plundered is the Canaan with every evil—Askelon is carried off—Gezer is seized—Yenoam is made as though non-existent—Israel is desolated, her seed is not—Kharu (South Palestine) has become a widow—all lands are united, and pacified; everyone that is turbulent is bound by King Mernepthah."

The interpretation of this tablet appears to be, that the principal object of the expedition is claimed to have been achieved—the Hittite land in the north is at peace. The remainder refers to what Mernepthah claims to have done on the way there. It seems evident from a map of Palestine, that the Egyptian army followed the coast corridor route along the shore of the Mediterranean by Askelon and Gezer, and penetrated inland, before reaching Mount Carmel, to the key position of Yenoam on the Jordan, immediately below the Sea of Galilee, which his predecessor had also occupied. The juxtaposition of Israel to Yenoam on the stele, places them in the north, near the Plain of Esdraelon, the scene of Deborah's victory, which, as will shortly be seen, probably took place soon after this event. The pacification of the south of Palestine apparently by brutal methods on the return journey, completes the record. Indeed, regarding the inscription as a whole, one gains an impression that it records a campaign of massacre and plunder in Canaan, and a treaty of peace when the Hittite country was reached, with that nation.

Whatever may be deduced from the silence of the Bible regarding this campaign, it is evident that it took place when Israel was already in occupation of Canaan; and its record is fatal to the claim that Mernepthah was the Pharaoh of the Exodus. But if Joshua conquered Canaan nearly two centuries before this Pharaoh's campaign, how has it come about that all mention of Egypt, except in connection with the Exodus, is excluded from Joshua, Judges and the two Books of Samuel?

Several explanations have been suggested for this silence; these will be referred to later; but while they help us to understand, they do not entirely satisfy. There is an explanation so simple, and so complete, and indeed so convincing, that it is entitled to precedence.

Why is there this mysterious silence in the Sacred Narrative regarding the affairs of Egypt? If Egypt was ever mentioned in the original document, the scribes must have left it out of later copies. Why?

Long deliberation brings one to the conclusion that—
that is precisely what was to be expected!

Recall first of all how the references to the conquests of Canaan by Thotmes III, are disguised in the sacred narrative by the substitution of his badge—the hornet. Why such figurative language? Because all allusions to Egyptian aid, direct or indirect, *would dim the glory of the Exodus.* The Israelites, and their descendants the Jews, were never tired of recalling the Exodus from Egypt, and their deliverance from the Egyptians. The New Testament as well as the Old, testify to this fact. But beside all this, year by year, and every year, the Israelites, and later the Jews, celebrated their greatest Feast—the Feast of the Passover—to commemorate their deliverance from Egypt. How could Israelite scribes record the fact that Egypt was often their helper and protector within a century of that event? Or if the original document contained such a preposterous statement, is it not certain that later scribes would leave it out? How could they possibly transmit to posterity the fact that, despite the Exodus triumph, nevertheless Egyptian power had paved the way for Israel's entry into Canaan; and with the exception of Mernepthah's brutal raid, had often kept the peace for Israel's benefit after it was there. Historians who write from the patriotic standpoint are ever prone to disregard benefits received from other nations, and this history of Israel was written down by men who yearly celebrated their nation's deliverance from Egypt in the great Passover Feast; and who yearly renewed an intense religious exultation, in which Egypt played the part of the oppressor. This complete silence concerning Egypt for some centuries after the Exodus is a positive testimony to the fact that on the whole, Egypt helped Israel; and the very silence tends to further authenticate the Bible narrative.

The other reasons that have been suggested to account for the silence are as follows: The excavations of Jericho have familiarized us with the fact that though the city had big walls it was a little place. The Israelites were also a little people. Canaan, the Promised Land, was also a small country, no larger than Wales, and much more rugged and mountainous. Both Joshua and Judges contain admissions, like the one already quoted regarding Bethshean, that Israel could not always drive out the existing inhabitants. The occupation by Israel was therefore not complete, except perhaps in the Hill Country and Highlands.

The recognition that the through route between Egypt and the north passed along the seacoast, also helps to clear up matters. Once Israel was settled they became a pastoral or agricultural people. Even fourteen centuries later the Jewish historian, Josephus, could still write of his race:

"As for ourselves, therefore, we neither inhabit a maritime country nor do we delight in merchandise, nor in such mixture with other men as arises from it: but the cities we dwell in are remote from the sea, and having a fruitful country for our habitation, we take pains in cultivating that only." (*Against Apion*, I, 12.)

Thus the main body of the Israelites held aloof from the trade-routes; and there is plenty of evidence in Judges, that they only fought in the last resort, and lacked weapons of war, thus:

"Was there a shield or spear seen among forty thousand in Israel?" (Judges v. 8.)

It was Egypt's policy, on the other hand, to hold the coastland corridor for through communications with Syria and the north; both for purposes of trade and in order to defend itself on the plain of Esdraelon against invasions similar to those of the Hyksos.

Indeed the Hittites in the days of the Book of Judges had replaced the Hyksos in their menace to Egypt. That was why Bethshean, Yenoam, and Hamath, and Acco on the coast, were occupied by Egypt; and why it was important that Canaan, along whose shores lay the line of communications, should be at peace and even friendly to her. The fact that it was this coast corridor which was used by the Egyptians, left the interior of Palestine intact for the Israelites.

A summary of the contents of the Book of Judges throws further light on the absence of references to Egypt. Here is a book, covering a period of nearly four centuries, composed of folk-lore stories all pieced together, with long periods of rest between them.

Intervals of history are left unfilled which may once have contained glimpses of Egyptian intervention. Those who transmitted the Text probably said: "But why mention Egyptian help at all?"—The scribes were a religious body, therefore they cut out any allusions that may have been there, and salved their consciences with the thought that Egypt was but an instrument of the Lord God when she came to their assistance.

But though there are no direct references to Egypt, Professor Garstang has drawn attention to evidence of her presence and influence in the narrative recorded in the Book of Judges.

When the date Jericho has given us is used as a basis for the chronology of the Book of Judges, it is found that the periods when "the land had rest," coincide with the periods of time when Egyptian history represents the Pharaohs as exercising effective suzerainty over Palestine.

The author is specially indebted to Professor Garstang's *The Foundations of Bible History: Joshua, Judges*, for the following tables of comparisons between Biblical events and Egyptian events, with their approximate dates. There, set side by side, are summaries of events in Palestine and Egypt for the four hundred and forty years succeeding the Fall of Jericho, and they fit into each other. In studying the following tables it should be noted that this scale of comparison is made on an estimated date of 1440 B.C. for the Exodus of the Israelites from Egypt. The date suggested by Professor Garstang was 1447 B.C., or seven years earlier. The evidence advanced in this volume suggests that date as the earliest possible, the latest being 1437 B.C., or a margin of ten years. The author's preference, as will have been observed, is 1440 B.C. for the Exodus, and 1400 B.C. for the Fall of Jericho.

In his book on the subject Professor Garstang finds two other verifications of these chronological tables. The first is a statement of Jephthah, one of the Judges, to his neighbours the Ammonites:

"While Israel dwelt in Heshbon and her towns, and in Aroer and her towns, and in all the cities that be along by the side of the Arnon, three hundred years? why therefore did ye not recover them within that time?"   (Judges xi. 26.)

This presumes a period of three hundred years after the time of Joshua to Jephthah, which is justified by this chronology.

The other is earlier, and occurs in the celebrated Old Testament poem, the Song of Deborah:

"In the days of Shamgar the son of Anath, in the days of Jael, the highways were unoccupied, and the travellers walked through byways."   (Judges v. 6.)

The allusion is to a time when lawlessness and violence had compelled peaceful travellers to take to the less frequented camel tracks.

A text in an earlier chapter refers also to Shamgar the son of Anath—otherwise Shamgar Ben Anath:

"And after him was Shamgar the son of Anath who smote of the Philistines six hundred men with an ox goad; and he also saved Israel."   (Judges iii. 31.)

A reference to the chronological tables will reveal the fact that Shamgar lived in the days of Rameses II.

One of this Pharaoh's sea captains was Ben Anath; he was a Syrian by birth, and became the husband of one of the daughters of Rameses II. Thus he may be one and the same person with the Israelite Judge— Shamgar Ben Anath. It is suggested that the weapon, used for slaying the Philistines, was a ship named *The Ox Goad*.

Professor Garstang's comparisons between the events recorded in the Book of Judges and in Egyptian history are set out on the two next pages.

Name of Leader	B.C.	Space of Time	The Bible Story	The Egyptian Story
Moses . . .	Between 1447 and 1437, say 1400	40 years	Wandering in the Wilderness.	Egyptian invasion and domination of Palestine.
Joshua . .	1400 to 1360	40 years	Invasion and penetration of Palestine.	Egyptian apathy and Habiru revolt (see Tel el Amarna letters).
(Cushan) .	1360 to 1352	8 years	Israel oppressed by Hittites.	… …
Othniel . .	1352 to 1312	40 years	Rest.	Egyptian domination.
(Eglon) . .	1312 to 1294	18 years	Oppression of Eglon, king of Moab.	Egypt occupied with various rebellions.
Ehud . . .	1294 to 1214	80 years	Rest. Period of Shamgar.	Egyptian domination by Rameses II. The Mernepthah stele.
(Sisera) . .	1214 to 1194	20 years	Oppression of Sisera	Anarchy in Egypt.
Deborah . .	1194 to 1154	40 years	Rest.	Egyptian domination by Rameses III, etc.

Name of Leader	B.C.	Space of Time	The Bible Story	The Egyptian Story
(Midianites) . .	1154 to 1147	7 years	Midianite oppression.	Egypt's power declines.
Gideon . . .	1147 to 1107	40 years	Rest.	
Abimelech . .	1107 to 1104	3 years	...	
Ammonites . .	1104 to 1103	1 year	Oppression.	Withdrawal of Egypt.
Jephthah . .	1103 to 1098	6 years	Israel had occupied Heshbon 300 years.	
(Philistines) and Samson 20	1098 to 1058	40 years	Philistine oppression.	
Eli . . .	1058 to 1038	20 years	Philistine oppression.	Philistine domination.
Samuel . .	1038 to 1018	20 years	...	
Saul . . .	1018 to 1003	15 years	Monarchy.	
David . . .	1003 to 963	40 years		Relations with Amenemopet.
Solomon . .	963 to 960	4 years	...	Siamon.
		482 years		

XIX

THE EVIDENCE FROM TELL DUWEIR
(LACHISH)

TELL DUWEIR is one of the largest ancient sites in Palestine; it is situated in the low hill country of Judah about thirty miles south-west of Jerusalem, and fifteen miles west of Hebron. From its summit one looks west right out over the Philistine Plain to the blue waters of the Mediterranean, a distance of about twenty miles.

The Tell is surrounded by rugged hilly country, and forms part of a ridge of foothills which creates a natural barrier, and separates the interior of Palestine from the coastland corridor of fairly level ground that runs from Gaza to Carmel. The excavation of this great Tell was commenced in the winter of 1932–3 by a joint British and American Expedition, and continued during the winter 1933–4 by the Wellcome Archæological Research Expedition to the Near East, both under the leadership of Mr. J. L. Starkey. A surprising amount of progress has already been made in the excavations, taking into consideration the vast area to be examined. Some of our readers may be puzzled by the association of this mound with the Biblical city of Lachish; for it will be remembered that a site named Tell el Hesy was long ago excavated for the Palestine Exploration Fund, and assumed to be Lachish. Since the War, however, there has been a consensus of opinion that Tell el Hesy marks the site of the Biblical city of Eglon, and that the great mound of Tell Duweir must be the far more important city of Lachish. The excavations up to date favour this identification.

A passing reference must now be made to Sennacherib, the great king of Assyria, who ruled 704–681 B.C. Dr Frankfort, excavating on behalf of the Chicago Oriental Institute, has recently found remains of the canal by which this king conveyed water from the Gomel river to his city of Nineveh. The canal passed through tunnels and over aqueducts. Perhaps Hezekiah, king of Judah, had heard of it, when he cut an underground channel through Ophel, in order to bring the water of the Virgins Fountain inside Jerusalem.

Those who have visited the British Museum may recall the magnificent stone bas-reliefs that once adorned the walls of Sennacherib's palace at Nineveh. They depict the storming of Lachish by this Assyrian king in the days of Hezekiah, king of Judah. References to the siege will be found in 2 Kings xviii. 14–17, and Isaiah xxxvi. 2. Here, it may be mentioned, a bronze crest of a helmet has been unearthed in the ruins of Tell Duweir that is like the crests of the peculiar helmets worn by Sennacherib's spearmen on the bas-reliefs. This forms some slight evidence of identification.

In the excavation of ancient sites, remains of the last buildings, of course, come first. At Tell Duweir

THE RIVER GOMEL IN ASSYRIA

Showing where the entrance to Sennacherib's great canal aqueduct, from it to Nineveh, 30 miles away, has been blocked by a great mass of sculptured rock. Sennacherib reigned 705–681 B.C., and was contemporary with Hezekiah king of Judah.

(Courtesy of University of Chicago Oriental Institute.)

A RECONSTRUCTED PLAN OF THE CITY BELIEVED TO BE LACHISH

Which stood on the mound of Tell Duweir in South Palestine. Drawing by Mr. H. H. Williams, based on an oblique aerial photograph from the west, and plan of actual remains.

these included the residence of the Persian governor, which had been destroyed about 425 B.C. References are made to this Persian domination of Palestine in the Book of Ezra. It will be remembered that seventy years after the Jews had been carried into captivity by Nebuchadnezzar, they were permitted to return, and helped to rebuild Jerusalem by Cyrus, king of Persia. Cyrus, after destroying the Babylonian Empire (Dan. vi. 28), succeeded to its provinces which included Palestine. Next, the Expedition found the remains of the wall of the city built by Rehoboam, king of Judah (2 Chron. xi. 9), which bore evidence of having been breached by Sennacherib, 701 B.C., and later ruined by Nebuchadnezzar, 586–588 B.C. The examination of the remains of this wall brought to light some interesting evidence. The siege by the Assyrians under Sennacherib had been conducted on the lines depicted in the bas-relief, by assault and breaching. But Nebuchadnezzar and his army had used more brutal methods; they literally burnt their way through the walls where they had been repaired after Sennacherib's siege. To accomplish this, the Babylonians had cut down all the olive, fig and oak trees, that in those days covered the neighbouring hills, piled them with other combustible material against the repaired breaches, and set them on fire. The intense heat thus engendered reduced the limestone to powder, destroying large sections of wall. Thus the way was made for the entrance of the Babylonian army.

Bible students will remember that Lachish was captured by Joshua after he had defeated the five kings of the Amorites, headed by Adonizedek, king of Jerusalem. Japhia, king of Lachish, is stated to have been one of them, and the subsequent fate of the city is recorded in the following verses:

"And Joshua passed from Libnah, and all Israel with him, unto Lachish, and encamped against it, and fought against it; and the Lord delivered Lachish into the hand of Israel; and he took it on the second day, and smote it with the edge of the sword, and all the souls that were therein." (Joshua x. 31-32.)

Although the surface of the Tell has as yet been only partly excavated, the Expedition has carried out a great deal of exploration of its surroundings, and dug sections into its sides. A great number of rock cut tombs have also been opened in the surrounding valley, and the pottery, and other objects found inside them, have been examined.

With the aid of these it is possible to reconstruct some of the history of the place. It is surprising to be told that the greatest expansion of the city is estimated to have been about 3000-4000 B.C., or two thousand years before Abraham. Then the Tell seems to have been used as the citadel, or acropolis, of a much larger settlement, which, so far as can be judged at present, was without other defences. The next great change in the story appears at present to be marked by the characteristic Hyksos, or Shepherd King type of fortification, consisting of the sloping glacis and ditch. Cut into this glacis, and running parallel with it, are traces of a low subterranean tunnel, four feet wide, with a floor beaten hard by the passage of many feet. The tunnel recalled the wider and higher ones found at Old Gaza, which there ran into the Hyksos fosse. Mr. Starkey suggests that the Tell Duweir shafts were made and used by an Egyptian army besieging this city, in the course of expelling the Shepherd Kings from Palestine. The ascent of the formidable sloping earth ramparts, which nowhere afforded shelter from arrows or other missiles, was avoided by this method of attack. Once the passage inside, and parallel with the rampart, had been made, at a given signal it would have been easy to break through the interior side of the defences at many points, and to make a concerted entry into the city. Illustration of this form of attacking a besieged city by sapping has been found on Egyptian monuments. The Tell Duweir passage was, therefore, probably cut by Thotmes III in one of his great invasions of Palestine and Syria, or by an immediate predecessor. After the city had thus come under Egyptian control in the days of the early half of the eighteenth dynasty (1573–1473 B.C.) its prosperity revived. Houses were built again on the lower slopes of the Tell, and in the surrounding valleys, and here the account of these excavations grows in interest. People sometimes assume that excavation of the remains of an ancient civilization is a task in which the interest is sustained. But, like other walks in life, there is drudgery and discomfort, and even disappointment. These are endured in the expectation of what may be found. It is this anti-cipation, a form of speculation, which lures one on to further labour, or to spend more money. The soil of Palestine, as compared with that of Babylonia, or Egypt, or even Syria, has held many disappointments; so when, once in a while, important buildings are found whose contents have escaped the quest of a hundred generations of pillagers, it seems almost incredible, and the fact that it was made in the Holy Land itself, enhances the discovery.

Such a piece of good fortune now fell to the lot of the Wellcome Archæological Research Expedition. It took the form of the ruins of a small temple, built right outside, and below, the walls of the city on the filling of the Hyksos fosse. The excavators, when clearing the western slopes of the mound, came upon the thick walls of a building. In the east wall were niches, one of which contained no less than thirty-five bowls stacked in position. Further excavation to the west brought to light a blue glazed vase, and a few inches below it, *face upwards*, a very large scarab on which was engraved in eight lines of hieroglyphs, the already known lion hunt inscription of Amenhetep III, which read as follows:

"Live the Horus, the strong bull, uprising in Truth, Lord of the Double Crown, establishing laws, making ready both plains. Horus on Nubti, great and mighty, smiting the Setiu, King of Upper and Lower Egypt RA-NEB-MAAT, son of Ra, AMEN-HETEP HEQ UAST, granted life, and the royal wife TAIY who liveth. Reckoning of lions brought by His Majesty in

THE RUINS OF THE TEMPLE OF TELL DUWEIR (LACHISH)

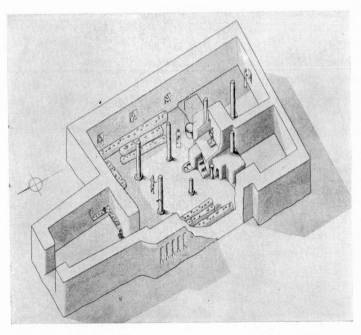

A RECONSTRUCTED PLAN OF THE TEMPLE, THE CONTENTS OF WHICH ARE
DESCRIBED IN THE LETTERPRESS

his shooting by himself, beginning in the first year up to the tenth year, lions terrible, 102."

(Petrie, Scarabs XXXI, 3.)

The name of this Pharaoh has already been so often mentioned in the pages of this book, that a particular interest is associated with this new discovery. It will be remembered that he reigned from 1413–1377 B.C., and that Jericho was captured by Joshua during this period. Since the tenth year of his reign would be 1403 B.C., it would seem evident that Lachish had not then been captured by Joshua.

In the course of the next two days, besides a large collection of objects in alabaster, faience, glass, and ivory, smashed into a thousand fragments, three more scarabs of Amenhetep III, of a smaller size, were brought to light. It now became obvious that the excavators had lighted upon a building of importance; and without stopping to record the further progress of the work, the following is a brief description of the complete find.

The building proved to be a small temple, about eighty-one feet long by forty-one feet wide. It consisted of an ante-chamber; the sanctuary itself with an altar on its south side; behind the altar a platform on which must have stood the image of the deity; and two small rooms at the back. An illustration of a reconstructional sketch of this temple is given here. It will be seen that three steps led up to the altar on its west side, and to the platform behind it. While ranged against the three other walls, north, east, and west of this sanctuary, were nine independent benches, made of solid brick, on which presumably the offerings of the worshippers were placed. The altar itself was also a solid block of square brickwork, three feet six inches high, and its steps enabled the priest to carry out the ceremonial toilet of the image on the platform.

But the astonishing part of the whole find was the way the temple furniture had been left undisturbed. There, on the left of the altar, sunk slightly into the floor, was a capacious round earthenware cauldron, some three feet in diameter, and rather more in depth, part full of pottery bowls, containing bones. On the other side, adjoining the steps, was a tall pottery stand and bowl for the drink offering. Alongside was an earthenware footbath for ablutions, and a decorated pottery censer for incense. The floor was strewn with quantities of pottery, and at the foot of the altar was a little curb, surrounding a small hearth, where charcoal would have been burnt for kindling purposes. The roof of the temple had been supported by oval wood pillars, their stone bases still remained, set in the plaster floor. The two rooms at the back were each about seventeen feet by thirteen. In the west one, a large collection of faience beadwork was found, which belonged to the Tel el Amarna period of decoration, 1400–1350 B.C., and included pendants of cornflowers, of mandrake fruit, of daisies, etc., together with fragments of glass perfume vessels. On the north and east exteriors of the building were circular pits, which had been used for the temple rubbish. These held quantities of bones, the remains of offerings, and pieces of worn temple furniture and decoration. There was a miniature face in ivory of excellent workmanship, and a beautiful outstretched ivory hand, of delicate proportions and refinement, about two-thirds life size. It would seem as though this hand had belonged to the temple image.

The refuse pits further yielded hundreds of beads and broken bowls; and among the latter, forty fragments of a ewer about one foot six high. These latter proved to be of great importance, for round the neck of the ewer, painted in red on a buff coloured slip, was the script to which reference has already been made. Below the writing as will be seen on reference to the illustration, one can distinguish a lion, a stag, gazelles, conventional trees, and perhaps a bird.

Among other ivory articles was a perfume flask, carved from a tusk. The flask is designed to form a lady wearing a long skirt; loop handles represent shoulders and arms; and on the slender body is a head, which served as a removable stopper. Through this ran a hole, connected with an open hand rising above the head, which served as a spoon.

On the wall paintings of the eighteenth and nineteenth dynasty tombs in Egypt, Syrians are depicted bringing such objects as this to the Pharaoh. When account is taken of Ahab's ivory palace at Samaria (1 Kings xxii. 39) some remnants of which were found by the British School of Archæology in Jerusalem in their recent excavations there; and when it is considered that the infamous Jezebel, Ahab's wife, was the daughter of a king of Sidon, it seems evident that Syria, or its coastland—Phœnicia—was the home of skilled workers in ivory. We recall too the verse in the famous forty-fifth Psalm: "Out of the ivory palaces stringed instruments have made thee glad" (v. 8), and the association of both David and Solomon with Hiram king of Tyre, and the traffic in ivory. But it is time to turn from these details, and to account for the presence of this temple outside the walls of an important Canaanite city, such as Lachish.

The presence of the Egyptian scarabs and the Tel el Amarna type of ornaments suggest that the temple had some connection with Egypt. Such a connection confirms what has already been recorded in previous chapters. Thotmes III conquered and effectively subdued Palestine, and the Tel el Amarna letters show that half a century and more later, in the days of this very Pharaoh, Amenhetep III and his successor, there were Egyptian governors in Palestine cities. The governor of Lachish was named Zimrida. Was this the chapel where he and those friendly to Egypt used to worship? Though the latest pottery of the temple just described is dated between 1295 and 1262 B.C., and there was also found a small pendant plaque in faience bearing the faint though unmistakeable cartouche of Rameses II (1295-1229 B.C.), it was also discovered that beneath the remains of the present building are those of an earlier one, as yet only partially uncovered.

In putting together what we know of the period, it seems probable that the earlier temple was destroyed by the Israelites under Joshua, and that the place was restored during one of the later dominations of Egypt, possibly at the time whem Shamgar ben Anath rescued Israel from the Philistines (see the end of the previous chapter).

If Professor Garstang's identification of Shamgar with the Ben Anath who married a daughter of Rameses II is correct, that alone would account for the revival of the temple, and the restoration of earlier treasures, such as the lion scarab of Amenhetep III, during Shamgar's time. Egypt must have lost influence in Palestine after Mernepthah's extermination of Israelites as recorded in his stele, and anything Egyptian would again have been marked for destruction. Such seems the best way to account for this temple at Tell Duweir; and anyway, it is noticeable what a fitting confirmation is given by this discovery, of conclusions reached long before it was found; as to the Jericho dates; to the evidence from Sinai; to the evidence from Tel el Amarna; and to the previous chapter on the Book of Judges.

One question remains to be answered which must have occurred to everyone who has read this chapter. How is it possible that the contents of this ruin appear to have been left undisturbed since the place was burnt more than three thousand years ago? In answer to this inquiry, Mr. Starkey finds evidence that its conflagration was followed immediately by torrential rains, which caused liquid mud from the slopes to pour into the now roofless fabric, and cover up the contents.

At a later date, when the city wall was rebuilt, the soil dug out for its foundations was thrown over the already buried ruin.

Little more needs to be said about the alphabetical script written round the neck of the ewer found in these temple remains. It is stated that the date of it must be between 1295–1262 B.C. It is acknowledged by all the leading authorities to be the connecting link between the alphabetical script, found at the temple of Serabit in the Peninsula of Sinai, and the script on the tomb of the Phœnician king Ahiram.

The several attempts to decipher the writing are recorded on the illustration. There seems no doubt that the first word is "gift." The suggestion of Father Burrows would dedicate the gift, or offering, to Shur, Mut and Alat—three deities whose names are associated together in this same order on the Ras Shamra tablets.

It is remarkable that the Ras Shamra tablets from Phœnicia represent an attempt to reproduce the Hebrew alphabet in the cuneiform script; while this ewer inscription reproduces it in the earlier Sinai script, which was afterwards adopted in Phœnicia. It would seem evident that the Ras Shamra people had heard of the alphabetical script in Sinai, and tried first to reproduce it in cuneiform.

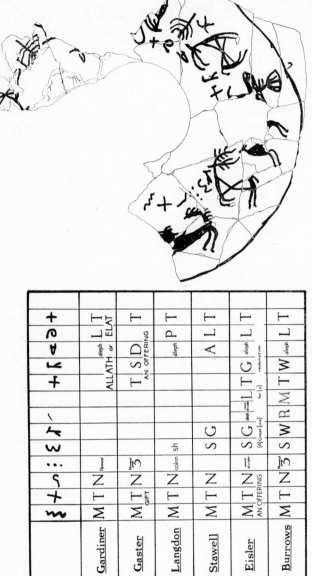

Gardiner	M T N (Numeral)			aleph L T / ALLATH or ELAT
Gaster	M T N (GIFT)	Numeral 3	T S D (AN OFFERING)	T
Langdon	M T N (colon) (sh)			aleph P T
Stawell	M T N	S G		A L T
Eisler	M T N (AN OFFERING)	S G (word divider) [A]Great [one]	L T G (aleph) (divider for [s]) (redemption)	L T
Burrows	M T N (Numeral 3)	S W R M T W		aleph L T

THE TELL DUWEIR SCRIPT AND ITS INTERPRETATIONS

The writing is painted round the neck of a ewer, mingled with conventional ornaments of a lion, a bird, giraffes and trees. It cannot be later than 1262 B.C. and is the connecting link between the Sinai and the Phœnician scripts.

CONCLUSION

THE task of completing this book has been facilitated by Sir James Jeans' recent address to the British Association. For this present volume has been written with, at least, some appreciation of the hesitation readers would experience in venturing to reject completely the so-called scientific criticism of the Old Testament. This difficulty naturally arises because the methods of that criticism, as well as its conclusions, had received the sanction and approval of a great body of scholars and divines. What qualification, therefore, could any layman possess for questioning such authority? The task was made harder, because it is obvious that those who seek a clearer understanding and interpretation of the Bible, deserve every sympathy and encouragement. And such a desire undoubtedly impelled many to accept and apply to the Bible the methods of a materialistic school of thought, which it is now evident were highly speculative; and which, while preaching impartiality, were both biased and one-sided. But the following sentences dissipate such doubts, and even may be said to place Science's seal of endorsement and approval on the course that has been pursued in this work. The words to be quoted apply to the Science of Physics, a science which, perhaps more

263

than all others, has had the benefit of experience to verify its conclusion. How much more do they apply to the so-called scientific criticism of the Bible, which has either passed from strength to strength, or from error to error, without any verification, for the critics have been a law unto themselves. Here then are the words of the President of the British Association :—

"The theoretical physicist must admit that his own department looks like nothing so much as a building which has been brought down in ruins by a succession of earthquake shocks. The earthquake shocks were new facts of observation, and the building fell because it was not built on the solid rock of ascertained fact, but on the ever-shifting sands of conjecture and speculation." (*vide The Times*, 6th September 1934.)

The new facts of observation, in the case of the Bible are the archæological discoveries of the last ten years; and their effect upon the edifice of erudition, erected by the scientific criticism of the Old Testament, also resembles a series of earthquake shocks. Likewise this edifice is also in ruins, because it was not built on the solid rock of ascertained fact, but on the ever-shifting sands of conjecture, and speculation.

Nor must it now be overlooked, that the collapse of this school of thought, releases every book in the New Testament, as well as the remainder of the Old, from the cloud of materialistic doubts and uncertainties, which have been poured on them ever since this century began, and have dimmed their messages to some of our ablest minds.

CONCLUSION

If the affirmative side of all the new evidence is now considered, the broad conclusions to be derived from it, undoubtedly testify to the validity of the Old Testament narrative. And the comparison becomes the more convincing, because at times the new evidence conflicts, not with what the Bible actually says, but with what has been read into it. For example, the small size of Jericho; or the Egyptian protection accorded to Israel in the days of the Judges.

But so far as the contents of the Old Testament in its original Hebrew are concerned, a comprehensive survey of the evidence left behind by these contemporaries of Noah, Abraham, Moses, Joshua and Hezekiah, shows that what has been found, is both consistent with that sacred narrative, and in confirmation of it. For example:

1. The ground has been cleared of all the prejudice, created by unsound criticism against traditional interpretation of the archæological evidence.

2. There is the evidence, from those most ancient libraries of cuneiform tablets, that Monotheism was the original religion. And there is confirmation of this great fact from other sources, especially from the Science of Anthropology. Along with this is the evidence of a universal belief in a Future Life.

3. The evidence that the stories of the Creation, the Temptation, the death of Abel, the Patriarchs before the Flood, and the Golden Age, were widespread and well known in the time of Abraham.

4. The proof that the art of writing existed before the Flood; and was practised in quite a number of forms after the Flood right down through the ages.

5. That alphabetical writing was certainly in existence in the Peninsula of Sinai when Moses led Israel there out of Egypt. And that the same alphabetical writing was introduced into Palestine, and was in use there not long after the days of Joshua.

6. The evidence for the Deluge, and the Dispersion from the Caucasus.

7. The testimony of the early advanced civilization in Asia and Asia Minor; and especially in Ur of the Chaldees, the actual home of Abraham.

8. The geographical correctness of the Books of Genesis and Joshua, as well as the chronological correctness indicated by pottery fragments on the various sites.

9. The testimony that Semitic civilisation from the Euphrates valley, and later, Hyksos from there and Arabia, conquered and occupied Palestine before Abraham, and that Canaanites and Amorites were fellahin precisely as indicated in Genesis 9. Thus the country was called "the land of the Hebrews."

10. The Ras Shamra evidence of Arabs speaking archaic Hebrew in South Palestine in confirmation of the above, and further, of mysterious rites in the wilderness of Kadesh many centuries before Moses and the Israelites lodged there.

11. The identification of professional soldiers, called Habiru, in Babylonia and Assyria about 2200 B.C. (Abraham born 2160 B.C.) with Hebrews.

12. The Keret tablet found at Ras Shamra which at least indicates, that a Chaldean chief named Terah left Ur of the Chaldees with his people and migrated to Northern Syria, and that later his people penetrated into Palestine, and associated with the story the names of Zebulon and Asher.

CONCLUSION

13. The correctness of the chronology of the Old Testament from Abraham to Rehoboam, when based on the Jericho dating; and actually verified by the astronomical date of Hammurabi's (Amraphel) reign at one end, and by the Egyptian date for Shishak at the other (see Chronological Table next the Index).

14. The archæological evidence associated with the raid of Chedorlaomer, king of Elam, and with Melchizedek, king of Salem.

15. The other evidence that goes to establish the historical reality of Abraham, Isaac, Jacob, Joseph and Joshua.

16. The surroundings of Moses' early life in Egypt as supplied by Egyptian history in the light of the Jericho chronology.

17. The evidence from the temple of Serabit, beautified by Princess Hatshepsut, and in that same Peninsula of Sinai to which Moses led the twelve tribes of Israel.

18. The Ras Shamra tablets testimony to the existence of imitations of the Mosaic Ritual, both as regards sacrifices and as regards the use and service of a tabernacle form of worship. This discovery is the more startling because the date assigned by the French experts to the tablets is immediately after Moses.

19. The frequent mention of the Divine names El and Elohim, and the mention of Yah on the Ras Shamra tablets, and the confirmation given to the writings of Sanchuniathon, who mentions El Elyon. In this connection, there is also Dr Langdon's testimony for the use of Elohim by the Habiru, or Hebrews as far back as 2200 B.C.

20. The evidence of the Jericho excavations, the walls fallen flat outwards, and untouched foodstuffs in

the burnt city, in exact confirmation of the book of Joshua.

21. The further evidence from Ai and Hazor for their destruction about 1400 B.C.; and the accuracy of the geography concerning the surprise attack on the former place.

22. The confirmation accorded by the Tel el Amarna letters, written at this same period, which mention the Habiru invasion, and even the very name of Joshua.

23. The silence of the book of Judges about Egypt, and yet its chronological confirmation of that narrative with Egyptian history.

24. The evidence from Tell Duweir (Lachish) including the discovery of alphabetical writing that cannot be later than 1262 B.C. The general confirmation found among the ruins of the temple outside the walls, with its scarabs of Amenhetep III. To which may be added the evidence concerning Rehoboam, Sennacherib, and Nebuchadnezzar, kings mentioned in the Old Testament at a later period.

Some of this evidence is conclusive in character. For example: The original Monotheism—the primeval civilizations—the general use of writing even before the Flood—the alphabetical writing at the time of Moses, first in Sinai then in Palestine—the whole Old Testament chronology proved to be correct from the time of Abraham to the founding of Solomon's temple, *verified by Astronomy at its very start in Abraham's time,* and again and again by later events even to Shishak's invasion in the fifth year of Rehoboam—the Ras Shamra testimony to the existence of the Mosaic ritual immediately after Moses—the complete confirmation of the Book of Joshua's account of the Fall of Jericho.

Such are the results of the last ten years. Is it not time to recognize what new reality they give to Christianity? And how they should breathe upon our dry bones!

It may be noticed that the references made in this work to the discoveries of the Science of Psychical Research, have not been summarized with the archæological results. In the course of this book they have been used to throw light on difficulties, rather than to testify to the correctness of the Old Testament narrative. Had the scope of this work included the prophetical books of the Bible, then they would have accorded valuable testimony. For the gift of prophecy or foretelling events, must be taken into account in any future attempt to revive criticism. And since the reality of the Unseen is now being recognized by Science, the constant contacts made with it in the Bible, can no longer be treated as delusions, or fairy tales.

Sir James Jeans' address on Science to the British Association, refers in the first instance to the Science of Physics; yet its implications and broad principles open up a far wider horizon. Science now recognizes that the Unseen is at least as important as what is familiar to us from the ordinary evidence of our senses. Thirty years ago Science laid stress on its Knowledge; to-day Science lays stress on its Ignorance. Thirty years ago the idea of so-called miracles was preposterous; to-day, miracles are possible; they are probable; they may almost be said to be certain. All life has become a miracle. Science has passed far beyond a mechanical conception of the Universe. Glimpses of unfathomable splendour are leading true Science to God.

If the study of the Bible is now approached from a similar standpoint, is there any doubt that it will be recognized as the Word of God in a much more real sense than ever before? The indirect effect of these archæological evidences upon the New Testament must be immense. Nor merely do they confirm the revelation of God to Moses, but they take us back before Moses to Melchizedek, and further. They even glimpse the mystery involved in such expressions as "the Lamb slain before the foundation of the world" (Rev. xiii. 8). But the evidence in favour of writings by Moses has peculiar importance for the following reasons:—Those who study the New Testament will recall that Jesus Christ's reply to the Temptations of the Devil in the Wilderness was to quote three passages from the Old Testament. All of these were taken from Deuteronomy, a book which critics had declared was composed many centuries after Moses. Yet that book repeatedly represents Moses as having uttered the words of this book. It seems as though no amount of explanation, or special pleading, can escape the issue, that from a critical point of view, the book was declared to be nothing more or less than a forgery. Is it conceivable that in answering the Devil, the father of Lies, Jesus Christ would have taken sentences from such a source?

CONCLUSION

Or again, and to conclude this work, we are confronted with Jesus Christ's statement:

"If ye believed Moses, ye would believe me *for he wrote of me*. But if ye believe not his writings, how shall ye believe my words?" (John v. 46, 47.)

From such a consummate dilemma, the archæological discoveries of the past ten years have already freed the Christian Faith.

What is real Science but a quest for the real Truth! Let us strive to disentangle ourselves from past conclusions of Science, which are proved today to have been falsely so called.

COMPARATIVE CHRONOLOGY OF EARLY BIBLE HISTORY

As Established by Excavations, and Verified by Astronomy and History

EGYPT		OLD TESTAMENT		BABYLON	
	B.C.		B.C.		B.C.
Xth Dynasty	2812-2627			Sargon	2751
XIth Dynasty	2627-2584			Naram-sin	2671
XIIth Dynasty	2584-2371			Sumu-abum	2169
XIIIth, XIVth, and XVIIth, contemporary with Hyksos Dynasties				Sumulailum	2155
		Abraham born	2160	Zabum	2119
XVth Dynasty	2371-2111			Apilsin	2105
XVIth Dynasty	2111-1583	Abraham entered Canaan	2085	Sinmuballit	2087
		Destruction of cities of the Plain	2061	Hammurabi (Amraphel)	2067
		Isaac born	2060	Samsuiluna	2024
		Jacob born	2000	Abiesuh	1986
		Jacob went to Egypt	1870	Ammiditana	1958
XVIIIth Dynasty		Israel in Egypt	1870-1440	Ammizaduga	1921
Aohmes	1573	Israel in Egypt	1870-1440	Samsiditana	1900
Amenhetep I	1560				
Thotmes I.	1539	Moses born	1520		
Thotmes II	1514	(Period of Hatshepsut)			
Thotmes III	1501	Moses fled to Midian	1480		
Amenhetep II	1447	Exodus from Egypt	1440		
Thotmes IV	1423	Wandering in Wilderness	1423		

Amenhetep III .	1413	Destruction of Jericho .	1400
Akhenaten .	1377	Conquest of Canaan under Joshua to .	1360
Semenkha .	1361	Israel oppressed by Hittites for 8 years to	1352
Tutankhamen .	1351		
Ay . .	1339		
Setymeramen .	1328		
Horemheb .	1322	Israel at rest for 40 years until . .	1312
XIXth Dynasty			
Rameses I.	1318		
Sety I .	1317	Israel oppressed by Moab 18 years to .	1294
Rameses II .	1295	Shamgar ben Anath, and **80 years' rest** to	1214
Mernepthah .	1229	(Mernepthah's raid)	
Sety II .	1210		
Amenmesu .	1205		
Tausert .	1204		
Arisu .	1197	Oppression of Sisera 20 years to .	1194
Sepnekht .	1196		
Rameses III .	1195		
Rameses IV .	1163		
Rameses V .	1157	**40 years' rest** to	
Rameses VI .	1153		1154
Rameses VII .	1145	Midianite oppression 7 years to .	1147
Rameses VIII .	1138		
Rameses IX .	1137		
Rameses X .	1137	Gideon 40 years to .	1107
Rameses XI .	1118		
Rameses XII .	1112	Abimelech 3 years to .	1104
Smendes .	1083	Ammonite oppression 1 year .	1103
		Jephthah 6 years to .	1098

S

COMPARATIVE CHRONOLOGY OF EARLY BIBLE HISTORY—continued

EGYPT		OLD TESTAMENT		BABYLON
	B.C.		B.C.	B.C.
Psusenes . .	1057	Samson, and Philistine oppression 40 years to	1058	
		Eli, and Philistines 20 years	1038	
		Samuel 20 years to	1018	
Neferkheres .	1011	Saul 15 years to .	1003	
Amenofthis .	1007	} David 40 years to	963	
Osochor .	992			
Psinaches .	975	Solomon's 4th year (founding of temple)	959	
Psousennes .		Rehoboam .	923	
Shishak .	940	Fifth year .	919	
Usarken I .	919			

The Babylonian dates on page 272 are from the Venus Tablets of Ammizaduga.

The Egyptian chronology is from Sir Flinders Petrie's "Revision of History" (*Ancient Egypt*, March 1931). This chronology was made on a basis entirely independent of that of the Jericho dating, which Sir Flinders did not even accept. Nevertheless, these Egyptian dates fit into the Old Testament chronology based on the Jericho dating. In particular, attention is drawn to the eighty years' rest commencing in the second year of Rameses II, and to the forty years' rest commencing in the second year of Rameses III: while the fifth year of Rehoboam, when he paid tribute to Shishak (1 Kings xiv. 25, 26) coincides with the last year of that conqueror's reign.

Jephthah's statement that the Israelite occupation of Transjordania extended to three hundred years (Judges xi. 26) furnishes a further check on the date of 1400 B.C. for the destruction of Jericho, as does, of course, the 480 years for the date of the Exodus (1 Kings vi. 1) from the fourth year of King Solomon.

INDEX

A

Aahmes, Queen, 179
Abanah, 116
Abdkiba, 231
Abel, 58, 219, 220, 265
Abiesuh, 114
Abimelech, 131, 250
Abraham, Abram, 7, 22, 45–49, 52, 58, 63, 69, 85, 87, 89, 96, 97, Chapter IX, 180, 187, 188, 210–212, 220, 226, 254, 265, 268; birth, 70; belief, 29; burial, 49, 137; dates, 55, 71; genealogy, 27, 57, 83, 105–107, 209
Accadians, 60, 77
Acco, 245
Acre, 37, 240
Adam, 97, 219, 226
Adam (city), 159
Admah, 90, 122
Adonis, 235
Adonizedek, 127, 253
Æschylus, 62
Æsculapius, 99
Africa, 35, 73, 92, 181
Agade, 87
Agzarim, 102
Ahab, 151, 216, 259
Ahiram, 92, 261
Ahiyami, 227
Ai, 119, 130, 145–147, 182, 268
Aiah, King of Pella, 234
Aion, 97
Akaba (Aqaba), Gulf of, 40, 43, 44, 93, 175, 186, 187, 189, 191, 207
Akhenaten, Akhenaton, 154, 166, 169, 229–231, 235, 237, 238

Alat, 262
Albright, Dr., viii, 45, 82, 119, 120, 122, 128
Allenby, Lord, 40, 85, 138
Alphabetical script, v, 29, 49, 50, 92, 93, 193, 194, 197, 211, 261, 266, 268
Amalekites, 121
Amenemket III, 194
Amenemopet, 250
Amenhetep I, 169, 179, 181
Amenhetep II, 169, 171, 174, 175, 182, 183, 231, 236
Amenhetep III, 154, 166, 169–172, 174, 194, 201, 231, 235–238, 256, 257, 260, 268
Amenhetep IV (Akhenaten), 229, 231, 235, 237, 238
Amenmessu, 240
Amenophis, 175
America, 47, 118
Ammiditana, 114
Ammizaduga, 113, 114
Ammonites, 247, 250
Amorites, the, 27, 28, 49, 53, 89, 90, 122, 233, 237, 253, 266
Amraphel, 113, 121, 122, 127, 267
Amurru, 28, 90
Anath, Ben, 247
Ancient Egypt (Petrie), 34, 71, 76, 81, 101, 169, 172
Anglo-Saxon History, 51
Animism, 25, 60
Anthropology, 25, 29, 63, 64, 221, 265
Antiquities (Josephus), 115, 180
Aohmes I, 168, 169
Arabah, 86, 96, 207

275

INDEX

C

Cabiri, 99, 102
Cadiz, 92, 102
Cain, 219
Cairo, 186
Cairo Museum, 239
Cambridge Ancient History, 171
Canaan, 84, 89–92, 105, 107, 112, 115, 117, 119, 173, 174, 180, 183, 203, 209, 210, 213, 229, 232, 233, 236, 242, 243–245
Canaanites, the, 27, 28, 29, 35, 36, 41, 53, 55, 60, 89, 94, 99, 209, 237, 259, 266
Canadian Law Courts, the, 18, 19
Cappodocians, the, 102
Carmel, Mount, 36, 37, 189, 241, 251
Carnarvon, Lord, 238
Carter, Mr. Howard, 238
Carthage, 92
Caspian Sea, 72, 75
Caucasus, the, 33, 71–75, 266
Chaldea, 209
Charran, 118
Chedorlaomer, 121, 122, 124, 267
Chenet, M., 48, 200, 211
Chicago Oriental Institute, 252
China, 62
Close, Sir Charles, ix
Colchians, the, 75
Comparative Religion, 63
Cornwall, 92
Corybantes, 99
Creation, the, 58, 98, 265
Crete, 131, 132, 202
Crookes, Sir William, 119
Crusades, the, 186
Cuneiform writing, vii, 22, 25, 26, 28, 47, 48, 50, 51, 58, 60, 64, 67, 70, 71, 85, 88–90, 93, 98, 109, 110, 111, 113, 114, 198, 200, 202, 211, 218, 227, 230, 239, 262, 265
Cushan, 249
Cypro-Phœnician Ware, 162, 166
Cyprus, 50, 102, 200–202
Cyrus, 252

D

Damascus, 43, 44, 115–117, 124
Dan, 35, 102, 124
Darius, 85
David, 31, 55, 136, 156, 157, 217, 225, 233, 250, 259
Dead Sea, the, 28, 39, 40, 43, 45, 97, 120–123, 128, 130, 142, 148, 159, 207, 210
Debir, 82
Deborah, 145, 227, 242, 247, 249
Deeks, Miss, 18–21
Deluge, the, 33, 58, 67, 69–72, 75, 266 (*see also* The Flood)
Deluged Civilization of the Caucasus Isthmus, The (Fessenden), 71
Dioscuri, the, 99
Dispersion, the, 33, 67, 72, 75, 77, 266
Divinity of Christ, 4
Dodanum, 101
Dog River, 241
Dothan, 119
Doyle, Conan, 50
Driesch, Professor Hans, 119
Driver, Canon, S. R., 23, 24
Dushratta, King of Mitanni, 235
Dussaud, M. René, viii, 117, 207
Dyaus-Petar, 62

E

Ea, 227
Eber, 105–107
Eboracum, 168
Ed, 206
Edom, 175, 177, 209
Edomites, 108, 128, 176, 177
Eglon, 249
Eglon, city of, 252
Egypt, v, 26, 27, 35, 80–83, 85, 88, 89, 91, 99, 100, 101, 111, 112, 138, 144, 167, 169–174, 176, 179, 180, 183, 184, 186, 192, 213, 229, 231, 239, 242–246, 249, 250, 255, 259, 260, 266–268

INDEX

Gerar, 80, 90, 119, 130, 131
Gezer, 194, 241
Gideon, 190, 250
Gilead, Mount, 116, 122
Gizeh Museum, 230
Gladstone, Mr., 1
Glueck, Dr. Nelson, 175, 176, 187
Gomel, River, 252
Gomer, 101, 102
Gomorrah, *see* Sodom and Gomorrah
Gordon, General, 39
Goshen, 181
Grant, Dr., 194
Greek Mythology, 75, 97
Greeks, the, 86, 102

H

Habiru, the, 106, 108, 210, 231–233, 249, 266–268
Hagar, 127, 128, 185
Hai, 118
Haifa, 37, 39
Ham, 41, 72, 73, 75, 86, 90, 123
Hamath, 240, 245
Hamites, the, 74
Hammurabi, 113, 114, 122, 127, 212, 267
Ha-Nebu, 101
Haran, 107, 108, 114–117
Hathor, 191, 192
Hatshepsut, Princess, 154, 166, 174, 178–181, 191, 196, 231, 267
Hauran, 43, 44, 115, 123
Hawwa, 97
Hazor, 82, 143–147, 268
Hebrew Alphabet, 8, 262
Hebrew language, 7, 28, 51, 84, 87–89, 198, 202, 203, 205, 222, 266
Hebrew script, 198
Hebrew Union College, Cincinatti, 175
Hebrews, the, 25, 57, 60, 83, 84, 87, 106, 107, 117, 232, 233, 266, 267
Hebron, 49, 132, 137, 138, 251
Hedjaz, 43

Hermes, 99
Herod, 149
Herodotus, 21, 75, 93, 94
Heshbon, 250
Heth, 90
Hezekiah, 125, 212, 252, 265
Hibbert Journal, 225
Hiel, 151
Higher Criticism, vi, 12–15, 21, 29–31, 67, 74, 196, 197, 224
Hilprecht, Dr., 10, 67
Hiram, 94, 259
Historical Criticism, 13, 14, 21, 29, 30
Hittites, the, 36, 41, 48, 49, 137, 201, 202, 231, 232, 239, 241, 242, 245, 249
Hobab, 190
Holy Land, the, 31, 53, 120, 255
Horeb, 188, 189, 192, 226
Horemheb, 238
Horites, the, 41
Hrozny, Dr. F., 49
Huleh, Lake, 143
Hurrians, the, 41
Hyksos, the, viii, 27, 28, Chapter VII, 79, 80–85, 88–90, 100, 101, 124, 135, 143, 144, 150, 154, 162, 166, 169, 180, 181, 201, 213, 233, 236, 245, 254, 256, 266
Hypsistos, 61, 125

I

Ianhamu, 234
Iberians, the, 102
Ilah, 60
Illani, 106
Illustrated London News, 175
Imhotep, 99
India, 41, 62
Indian Ocean, 39, 44
Indo-European Group, 49.
Indra, 41, 236, 237
Intransigeant, 76
Inventions, 5
Iraq, 57
Ireland, 92, 100
Irwin, Rev. W. A., 1

INDEX

INDEX

INDEX

Printed in Great Britain
by T. and A. CONSTABLE LTD.
at the University Press
Edinburgh